# The Black Handbook for Corporate White America

# THE BLACK
# HANDBOOK FOR
# CORPORATE
# WHITE AMERICA

The real corporate journey
of a Black Leader

James Holley

**To order additional copies of this book, contact:**
Xlibris
1-888-795-4274
www.Xlibris.com
Orders@Xlibris.com
816640

# CONTENTS

Note to Executives....................................................1

Diversity and Inclusion...........................................9

White Privilege ......................................................12

Human Resources ................................................16
    *Recruiting*..........................................................16
    *Interviewers* .....................................................23
    *Performance Management* ................................23
    *Try A Different Approach* ................................26
    *Termination* .....................................................26

Coaching ...............................................................28
    *Group Coaching* ..............................................32
    *Are Blacks Really Coached?* .............................34

Get To Know Our Culture....................................36
    *Dress Code* ........................................................36
    *Pronunciation* ..................................................39

Black Music ..........................................................42
    *Role Models* ......................................................44
    *Get to Know Their Families*.............................47

Phrases to Stay Away from in The Workplace .............49
    *You All*...............................................................49
    *You're Not Like the Others*................................49
    *You Look Like So and So from That (Movie or Show)*..50
    *I Get Scared When I Get Pulled Over Too*....................51
    *I Was Poor Growing Up Too* ...........................52

*All Lives Matter, Not Just Blacks Lives* .......................53
*We Are All Discriminated Against* ..............................54
*Are You All Black (Meaning Mixed)?* .........................54
*Do You Play Sports?* .................................................55
*My Family Started with Nothing* ................................56
*Why Do There Need to Be Diversity Groups? What About
    White People?* ....................................................57
*Insinuating a Black Associate Is Friends with Another
    Black Associate* .................................................58
*Prettiest Black Girl or Most Handsome Black Man I
    Have Ever Seen* ..................................................58
*What Do You Think About the First Black Person That
    Did That? (Presidency, Entertainment, Etc.)* .........59
*I Love Rap Music* ....................................................60
*So Do Black People* .................................................60
*Things Have Gotten a Lot Better* ..............................61
*That Is So Ghetto* ...................................................61
*I Do Not See Color* .................................................62
*Oh, Your Husband or Wife Is Black?* .........................63
*I Have Black Friends* ...............................................63
Words Matter: ..........................................................65
Tips for Black Applicants ...........................................83
*Resume* ..................................................................84
*References* ..............................................................85
*Forget About the Perfect Job* ...................................87
*Stop Disqualifying Yourself* .....................................88
*Confidence and Personality* ......................................89
*Dress for Success* ....................................................90
*Get Some Rest* ........................................................91
*Research your Opportunity* ......................................92
*Greeting* .................................................................94
*Be Passionate* .........................................................94

*Take Your Time with Answers* .......................................96
*Interview Closure*.........................................................97
*Overcoming Snubs* .......................................................98
Summary: The Twenty-Six-Year Journey of a
Black Leader.................................................................100

*Dedicated to my super hero team of supporters.*

*To my amazing Mother and Hero. Your guidance and love has always kept me believing in what is possible. All I am is because of you.*

*To my Babydoll and beautiful wife. Thank you for being my strongest supporter. You are my partner in everything we accomplish and my rock. Most of all you are the reason I want to be a better man every day.*

*To my 7 brilliant children. Shante, Kashiya, Tarek, DeMarquis, Princess, Precious, and James Jr, you have sacrificed so much for Dad to lead the way I do and overcome all I have had to so that we could live a comfortable life. Everything I have done and will do, will be to honor you and continue to be the example of a Dad you can be proud of. Thank you for giving me 7 of the best reasons in the world to succeed with a full heart.*

*To my Brother Gate the Great! I did it my man...you always said I could.*

# NOTE TO EXECUTIVES

Please be very careful with the way you interact. Understand that the normal jokes that always been ok in these senior and executive level meetings are in fact deeply problematic. I wonder if you understand the confusion and discomfort of those few black senior managers or executives within the firm. Think about looking around and wondering what everyone is thinking, when all we are wondering is how we became the butt of the jokes or the men or women that do not belong. There is a real misunderstanding in larger corporations on what is ok to say and what is not, so they take a holistic approach to make sure they are not leaving anything out. If anything bothers you, make sure you report it to HR or to a manager. Are you sure you are comfortable laying down the law on what we think is racism, or have you just dotted the i's and crossed the t's? Just because you are a firm that has blacks in higher positions does not allow you to try to question our intelligence or bring out the old black jokes that you have been saving. The problem with having it so wide open is that people base their judgments on the acceptability of specific statements or actions on how it seems to impact the black person being spoken of. They watch to see if they seem upset. The answer to that is we have been upset by it since day one, but do not want to jeopardize your job? The job that no one else like you in the business has? The job that most people that we grew up with or know do not have?

Here is the depth to what it feels like. If you allowed a black man to work in the slave master's house it didn't always feel better because you were closer to the real root of the problem or heard more from those that didn't feel it was necessary back then to hide what was being said. Allowing us to become executives and bringing us closer to the top seems to be a way to make it extremely obvious that if there are fewer of us, we have to be extra careful. Some of that slave thinking is why the only black guy in the room smiles when an off-color joke is made. You put us in a situation where in order to provide for our families, we have to swallow insults and indignities with a smile. We cannot share it with friends because they will insist that we are a sell-out or that we should quit immediately. We allow more than we should because that is what we are used to. Most think our situation has improved, because we are no longer slaves. I say just because you cannot do the blatant things they would back then it still feels like we are not wanted or do not belong. It makes us question our abilities. It makes us question whether we should be in that position or whether we should apply for a senior position if one opens up. We are not still walking in the same footsteps as our ancestors and there are regulations in place that supposedly make us feel better or protected. But let me ask a question. In most cases HR will talk about retaliation and their no retaliations policy. They will also keep your information confidential. Here is the other side to that. If I am a black man and the only one in the company who do I tell without others knowing it was me? You feel as if your actions protect everyone, when they really only protect you. We are quiet at times, especially when there is just one or a few black people in a meeting on a regular basis. Maybe this is because we do not want to step on toes or ruffle feathers. Again the thought of going back to where you grew up will make you think long and hard about the things you dispute or bring to light.

If those who dominate these meetings see the discrepancy then why would they think it is ok to bring out their old high school jokes and things like that so that the person feels even more alone? The worst part of this is that white people become so comfortable saying things that they would have never say to any other black person or would be too scared to walk into the hood and say. But the unbelievable stereotype of feeling as if you are around an intelligent black man or woman who has abilities that other black people do not, and who will therefore accept some of the racism because they do not live where others do, or got better schooling than most do, is ridiculous. This is the clearest form of racism there is. Those who think it is ok because someone doesn't speak up or say anything about it. Let's be honest we feel outnumbered which means that if we report it and the other five people in the room were white then it is our word against theirs. Now stack the odds and consider why if we are always outnumbered we are truly never heard or silenced because no one else will say something.

We are not talking about Colin Kaepernick because he kneeled we are talking about him because he is black and kneeled. This proves that even though he is considered the leader on his team at the quarterback position he still could not get one white teammate to do it. Now if a white person would have done this first the others that saw it would not be as likely to speak out the way they did. A black person is trying to make you aware of the fact that there are social injustices that everyone knows about and you are looking for what he is disrespecting instead of the true reasoning which let's be honest was already known and heard long before he kneeled. So he was the star of the team but when it came down to it he could not get his white teammates to follow him into something that could help change based on the platform that he had as an NFL quarterback. Even in a league where over 80% of players are black. Some did it on other teams others that are white started to join in so the conversation got legs and others started to listen. I used this example to prove the point of that no matter your stature people still do not want you to speak out about things that they know are wrong. The biggest part of that example is that he still does not have a job. A Pro Bowl player who went to the Super Bowl literally got banned due to the power of the white owners in the NFL who honestly do not know how to treat those who are the dominating force to their product. It reminds me a lot of our government. If he loses his job or is persecuted what are we supposed to think will happen to us?

I honestly think it is a tactic used at times to run blacks out of the business. How much can we take before we just quit and "go back where they we came from" or before we become what they like to call egregious or violent which would cause us to lose our job for insubordination? If we complain about why there are not more of us in the organization they consider us entitled. If a white person complains about it to all of the others that look just like him it will cause conversation and if that is what it takes. I am all for it. You're only my friend if you can be just as honest with those around us as you are with me and not just on your visits to the hood.

Organizations spend so much time trying not to specify what exactly is ok or not they miss the big picture. We need to be trying to holistically solve a problem that has been around for generations. If you become more open to equality as a whole it may change the way you operate day to day. If you stop thinking that one of us magically prepares ourselves for an opportunity that we get and others do not you may realize that if you will not be honest about the shortcomings of hiring black candidates within your organization then it will always be the case that you will only be seeing one or two black men or women across the table. If everyone is scared to say it is not a good look or that statistics show that more training or resources might be necessary for a black person to be successful compared to someone of a different ethnicity and you do not provide those resources, then you're not looking for diversity within your organization you're looking for brownie points for hiring one or you use the few you have as tokens to try to prove that your organization is on board. This is the time where you're thinking, Are we supposed to go out of our way to treat them better than everyone else? The answer to that should be, "Hell yeah!". Especially since you know we have been treated unfairly for a very long time. But the real answer is no all we want is a fair chance and a fair organization to give us one. We are not expecting things to change tomorrow but we want to have the hope that they will.

The government has made some basic upgrades to some of what we can do now but they will never admit that up to this point our abilities and options have been hindered by a society that seems to keep telling us is in so many ways that we are not up for the challenge and not qualified. Even if you admit that you will not admit to how hard it was for us to achieve comparable levels of success and status as others. I wonder at times if people really think we do not want the opportunities or we want to continue to live in areas stricken by poverty. We want more and if you're willing to understand us more you may realize that we are a necessity to growth and prosperity even for your businesses and hey maybe we as blacks can grow and prosper in the process. It is easy to point the finger at a group and say they cannot do something but hard to admit that you're part of that problem and are not willing to be the organization that takes a stand to change the status quo.

Most executives new or old will talk about their success and if they are older we have to assume that they are used to fewer blacks being in the corporate world back then compared to now. So whatever new business they encounter, take over or are brought in to take over they hire the same cast of characters or look a likes and continue to run the new operation the same. However, what is not comfortable to you could be the best experience you ever encounter. It is a simple concept. If you really want diversity and inclusion within your organization then do not half ass accept certain regulations to adapt the fact that you are giving it the old college try. Be creative in your approach and a pioneer in the change that is necessary. If you want fewer blacks to be killed by policemen, hire more black policemen that will not be intimidated at the first sign of conflict or so uncomfortable or scared that they do not know how to calm the situation or understand the personality of those who have been obstacles to kick over for white police. If you want more blacks within your organization get a few more in the executive room, a few more black leaders, so that black employees feel more supported. If you want less crime and violence going on in the hood then show us the life that you have kept from us for so long, and make it real by not hiring a few to meet some arbitrary quotas. If you want us to be more educated, then why did you segregate schools back then and honestly is it is still happening to this day? The only difference is you have to be able to afford better living to be able to go to better schools otherwise we end up right where we have always been poor learning with high expectations. If you want more black teachers then tell the white teachers to stop geographically dismissing us when we are young or telling us based on circumstances that we cannot be whatever we want to be and honing our minds young so that we believe our standard is mediocrity. If these teachers give them hope and they become teachers even if it is a predominately black school they can give our black youth the sight and belief that it is possible and they will pay it forward tenfold to change the narrative of history.

If you want more black lawyers than put us in a position where we have the same abilities to achieve this, instead of black people only seeing one when they need representation. You cannot speak of why we do not achieve what one of your ten senior leaders do without making it clear that our opportunities and resources were not the same. Hope comes from seeing the masses succeed. What social achievement or movement has occurred that started and finished with one person? If we see more of them our vision changes and with the necessary resources it can change our plight of what we really expect from ourselves.

# Diversity and Inclusion

These are two words glorified by corporations. If you are aware enough as an organization to be a part of these programs then you are aware that they are necessary. You are also aware that the results have not changed much based on the company's efforts. Just because you say it out loud does not make it true. Camouflaging the approach and not measuring the results of your efforts just makes it another failed effort at something that already does not seem important enough and to some it will never be a priority. We should not have to wait for a diversity event to be able to see others like us in the organization. This is a sad approach. Put together programs so that our minority groups can be honest about the resources necessary for our people to be successful. More than that seek to be an organization that is open to learning and building the the diversity of your culture instead of being happy that you have programs in place that are not changing the outcome or success of them. How honest are you in those events about the past, heck even about our present? Hiring one black man or woman or promoting one is not your new flag to wave every time someone mentions it to you. Hiring or promoting one black person does not solve the problem of the unbalance in the corporate world right now. Can you as an organization speak out about your diversity efforts without the black employees now employed saying Where? How about those that come in for interviews that get a tour? Does it make you wonder what they think their real capabilities are or will be in your organization? That so-called "diversity and inclusion" turns into exactly what black people are already aware of "adversity and exclusion".

The real lesson here is that if you are doing it because you are mandated to or doing the bare minimum then the leaders of that organization should be ashamed. If there is a true plight to what you want to accomplish and you truly want to hang that diversity banner with pride then keep educating yourself around more ways to display your want and need for more diverse employees. Oh, and do not say it out loud to a black person unless you have a list of accomplishments so far or a solid plan to build a list. There is proof that more diverse companies perform better so why do most corporations still look the same? Think about the ideas you would get from different groups that come from different places and how that kind of insight can change the game. If you are surrounded by the same people all of the time, then professionally your mindset and thinking will be one-sided. We want to find ways to market to black professionals or business owners but we do not have anyone that looks like them to participate in the marketing tactics. The color of money is green and spends the same so why are we not allowing black brilliance to be a part of your company's breakthrough?

# White Privilege

This may be the most important aspect of the need for diversity in businesses. When you look around you're not surprised to see mostly white people. Seems like the norm so it is never really discussed but it seems to have the opposite affect when it is a black person. A black hire seems to turn heads or get discussion going not because you are racist but because it goes against status quo. The ability to know first is a lost skill. There are so many resources and so many stories out there it's hard to know what to believe. All we are asking is that you pay attention of what is right in front of you. Ask yourself if it is ok and if not, how you can help change it. Remember we are only asking for as much as you already have. If you will not at least own your white privilege status before you make general comments it is infuriating. If you will not allow yourself to admit that things are not equal it is selfish and cowardly. Those who take actions to speak out or even better take a stand will allow others to know it is ok to do so. Every corporation has a mission statement and a purpose. What does that mean if your actions do not justify that mission or purpose?

Think about specific situations. You have blacks who have the right to be outraged because of a young black man dying and the first thing you post or comment on is the looting that goes on after. If you see with your own eyes and you are still looking for reasons for it not to be true or trying to find something to make it more sensible to you, you are part of the problem. You have to see it for what it is. If a black man is killed by a cop and you say that you know a lot of good cops you are disregarding the black man who died by trying to justify it. You cannot call us violent because you are too scared to come to the ghetto and witness the love and togetherness that goes on as well. You cannot say most of us end up in jail because you will not go there to speak to them and find out that most should not even be there. You also know if it was your son or daughter they probably wouldn't be. You cannot say most of us are unemployed when you are doing nothing more to employ us. You cannot have one black friend that grew up near you and imagine that you therefore know all of us. You cannot speak to our tragedies but you can acknowledge our mistakes. You cannot live our lives but you can be a part of making them better. Most of all, you cannot be us but you can take the time to really see us as another person who should have all the same opportunities as the person standing next to them.

A lot of the above is more about white privilege as manifested in language and speech. You say things that you do not really mean and you are hoping we do not take it personal for that reason. The problem is if we say nothing it continues and gets worse. If we say too much we match the image of the man or woman that you stereotyped walking in the door. This was a hint for board meetings or other situations where the numbers of blacks are limited but they are expected to deal with nonsense like this. The rule has always been to exclude race, religion and politics from conversations in the workplace. The problem is there are too many people that build themselves around those things. Sometimes in good ways, sometimes bad. Those involved always outweigh the ones who are not involved, so you will never see the real statistics on discrimination because too many black people have to weigh their pride against the livelihood of their families. Remember, we do not always feel like there is intent. Most may be thinking I have heard far worse. I am trying to make a point at a minimal level that can skew to the positive moving forward. As I was saying the statements above are those who are just not educated enough about the situation or are one-sided regardless. That is another strong definition white privilege.

We do not blame you for feeling that way because of what you have experienced or not experienced for that matter. We get upset when you try to tip toe into a world you could never fully understand and make statements about one-off situations as if you are not aware of how bad things have always been.

If our respect really does matter then make a statement first about the unjust before you write one to condemn those treated unjustly. Think about the victim before you try to justify the reason for his being victimized. If you stand for what is right that is correct what is right. We do not want you to assume our stance we just want you to act and speak with enough knowledge and facts so that we stop justifying the means and put an end to them. Speak out because you know something is unjust or unfair. Acting as if it doesn't matter because it does not happen to you or your family does not give you a reason to stay silent. In every corporation there are regulations stating that even if you just overhear someone discriminating you need to report it. But in most cases even in real life we do not even speak out about it. It is easier to hide or walk away from it than to face the reality of the part you can play. We get it believe me and remember we are the ones that are being discriminated against. THINK ABOUT THAT. The clearest way to own white privilege is to simply to own the fact that you have more than we do!

# Human Resources

## Recruiting

I want you to think bigger than the government led or regulated programs that are necessary or mandatory. I am talking about doing what Human Resources specialists should do and that is open up their organizations to newer and fresher ideas of how to recruit and maintain talent. Black and brown recruits will not overwhelm you with schooling and prior experience, but they will overwhelm you with effort and hard work.

Recruiting and training need to work closer together so that there is an understanding of the help and training that will be needed to hire more blacks and diversify their businesses. We have to get away from looking for the perfect candidate which we still have not found. There are literally programs that businesses use to dictate the mood or behavior of the possible candidate. There are literacy and accuracy tests that are used before the interview happens. What you continue to tell black people is that we might as well not even apply. Literacy stats comparing whites and blacks already tell the story that everyone already knows and that is that the education system has failed black youth. So you justify that by allowing a literacy test that has a great chance of leaning toward a white candidate before a single conversation is had. We do not have to be around long to have seen the movies or read the books of our schooling compared to yours or our economic conditions compared to yours. The will we have to have to survive where we have grown up compared to yours. Someone has to start thinking differently about approaches and stop following every other organization that finds something that drops the attrition rate. Be bold and open in your conversations with black associates and leaders. Show them that you do care about our feelings and our culture. By narrowing down the field with these personality trait and literacy tests, you are minimizing the opportunity for black candidates that cannot help their educational plight but want more in life. It's like blaming our deaths on the fact that we were in the wrong place at the wrong time because we could only afford to live in poor or dangerous areas. I would have to assume that these things are discussed but I thought a guide from a black man that has been in the corporate world for over 26 years could give some real insight.

In your interviews you want to know the What but what you need to start to educate yourselves with and learn to understand is the Why. When you're setting parameters for the ability to join your company; are you considering the fact that those mandatory requirements are not possible for some as much as others? You should master your craft by researching the statistics for potential candidates that match what you are asking for. This way your organization can be a fix to the astronomical unemployment of blacks instead of the continued reason for it. We cannot overcome history or where we came from so why should we lose an opportunity for it? The lack of education isn't by choice, so be a company that provides schooling for those that need more education. Take the opportunity to do what others are not doing. Provide programs that will get those lacking the educational qualifications to gain the necessary knowledge. If we need it to compete, and you will not provide it, then we are back to square one, and that is DENIED. The problem is that is not the first or the second or even twentieth time that we have felt that kind of rejection.

Then you have the predictive scores that give you the ability to make more decisions before there is a conversation. If you want to use these as qualifications, then you need a model that can measure black people vs white. For instance how do you expect someone working for a bank vs someone who was a waitress to feel based on their last job? The only way you can reasonably think that using the same predictive model without demographic or racial data is impossible. You know why no one will do it because the risk is not worth the reward. I get it. I get it. It is not ok to ask questions directly referring to a persons race. Then why do you still make decisions based on race? It's the lack of knowledge about your counterparts that allows it to continue. You think we are saying you make these decisions with racial intent. Well some do but the reality is we cannot make fully informed decisions without the information necessary to make an educated decision.

This is the main reason "wasted talent" was always spoken of in the hood because it wasn't always about the person wasting their talent. It was about how talented they were and it was wasted because of who they are or where they come from. If you could look at the statistics of how many blacks are interviewed compared to how many are hired it would paint the necessary picture. Maybe everyone needs the Rooney rule that the NFL uses where you have to interview a specific number of people for the open position. Although even in a coveted sport watched all over the world they still only seem to interview them knowing the backlash that comes from the same conversation every year. When you consider how many are turned away you're not even including the ones that cannot meet the requirements. They literally look at an ad for a job and have to cross it out. Now think about those that do not apply because they have been told their whole lives that they will not fit the requirements for most jobs out there and not having the means or resources to change that trajectory. This is on the large corporations to change the epic fail in terms of increasing the ability of jobs for black men and women.

It is the job of those who are fortunate enough to get into a powerful position to not be scared of sharing that power. They need to find new ways to distribute the ability to use that power in a way that others have been afraid of since long before my time using the guidelines set by the corporation to fall back on when decisions are made or risks are not taken. I think that as top executives you have to find it in yourselves to be accountable for your part in this. Just because you have the minimum of programs in place this does not necessarily make you an advocate. You all walk into rooms daily and look around and not see us, but you have become so blind to it no one ever asks. Then a black man or woman does join the team and there is a discomfort in the room that cannot be shaken. Out of sight out of mind. You have to start looking right in front of you and having the tough conversation about why your businesses are not able to recruit top black talent. That needs to be discussed whether there are any of us in the room or not. Because let's be honest one way or another when we are not around conversations are happening anyway and they are definitely not about how to hire more black people.

Corporations should start to look at work history in another fashion. Assuming you feel like you have been instrumental in building a strong training team any candidate that gets the job should be in good hands. Think about taking away the easy route of finding a candidate that has work experience within the field you are hiring. If it was that easy then it would not take a lot to be a recruiter. How can we be more creative in our approach?

Think about taking a different look at the experience and think about the qualities you are looking for in a candidate. Instead of assuming their experience is not strong enough to be successful think about it as a job and what it takes to be successful. Do those lower-level jobs prove that you have to be strong in mind as well as body? Do not allow a good, hungry candidate to get away because they did not have the same opportunities as others. The goal is to create a strong team that is open to new ideas and can be creative in ways that the company is not used to. These predetermined moves to lessen the necessary training and bring in those with the most experience are not always the best for longevity. If the black candidate worked in a restaurant for six years what do you think they would do in an a growing environment with continued opportunities?

Why are you paying trainers if you are looking for the perfect candidate with prior experience? How about the fight of attrition that large corporations continue to face? Using all of these predictive models that are based on those that have other opportunities at other positions. The desperate need of a black person to find employment is not just a constant journey but a constant feel of hope. Think about that every time you turn one down for lack of experience and look on the news and wonder why more tragedy occurred in the hood. You can only handle so much rejection before everything you have seen your whole life or have been trying to get away from comes to seem your only option again. When I think of attrition, I do not think of performance. I am on board with having performance metrics and performance management if the job entails that and it is measured fairly. The type of attrition I was used to after over fourteen years of senior management was voluntary. When you find the so-called perfect candidate with the perfect experience level and educational background we also have to understand that most competitors in our field are looking for the same. Here is where you think about lost resources due to training, hiring and re-hiring. If you continue to seek the same candidate as others in your industry then it becomes a revolving door from one organization to another. It is no longer about the best company, it is about paying the same candidates more money, which leaves the poor even poorer.

In no way am I saying take other black candidates and pay less. What I am implying is that if you would start using those resources and dollars to train and educate the black applicants that are not "as trained and educated" as you would like you could be the first organization to stop chasing the market value and begin building your own internal value. In doing that people start to understand that you are also building their brand, their future and the future of their families. That unfortunately is more than most black people could imagine growing up where they did. Invest in your people white, black, or brown it is the true future of all organizations. Believe in the people that stand in front of you not what you have seen on the news or who people are portrayed to be in movies or their music. Listen to the people who you are talking to and the passion in their voices.

Train your leaders and interviewers about being spontaneous and less scripted with their questions, so that they can adjust to what they see in resumes. Our minds are predetermined to look for exactly what we have posed as the best candidate. By doing this we remove the ability to see the possibilities and character that a black candidate can bring to the table vs their ability to do it RIGHT NOW. This is why we stay in the right now and continue to have to hire and re-hire, when we should be focused on training and retraining the associates we committed to growing.

# Interviewers

Try to see through the predetermined questions, and ask yourself by doing that always worked in the past. Do not just look at the resume for what you want to see. Look for what is unseen things that if explained more could give you a feel for what you are looking for without it jumping off the page at you. Study the resume as if every name you see has a chance. If your normal questions do not fit the norm or the experience seen on the resume be creative in how you ask. If you know the commitment it takes to be successful in your organization then simply ask what they think commitment means. If you know effort is necessary to achieve great things in your organization and you do not see anything to ask directly related to your industry just ask what they think hard work means? Black and brown candidates have wanted opportunities for a very long time. Their commitment to wanting that goes a long way. If we can take a moment to stop thinking about the best fit and just listen it will give you insight that you need. It can also help you in your next preparation for candidates that do not fit the mold whether white or black. If you disregard them for same reasons everyone else has then you are a part of the problem not the solution.

# Performance Management

I do believe in performance management. It is necessary to continue to gauge and grow. The issue is based on today's way of doing it. It has become a dreaded conversation for employees. A few things are necessary for these conversations to go well. The employee should not be finding out about the data used to have the conversation during the conversation. It should not be the first time they are hearing it because the ongoing improvement should be on the training and coaches. Holding those who teach accountable will help the acceptance of those who learn or expect to. Why are you not judging our leaders and trainers by the success of the masses along with the continued struggle by the same reps? You give them the ability to think in a well most of them are doing well. If that is the case then why not larger groups and say we will only be keeping ten of the fifteen in training? If you are going to disregard them do not allow them to see a future for six months or so and then pull the rug out from under them. If you want people who catch on faster or you have an organization that needs rep to reach a success rate fast then hire more or better trainers to make sure that happens. Attrition is just the root of the problem. If attrition is high it is better to focus on keeping employees on board.

We start watching videos to see how we can build better relationships with our reps. How you can step up our coaching efforts and build on inefficiencies? Once the attrition rate goes down the efforts go away. The consistency on how you attack our plight cannot get more intense and then go away. If that is the case, you will never get to a sustainable place or a real commitment to those you hire or who would like to be hired. I remember celebrations around three percent and I always thought Well what about the three percent lost. What could we have done better in those instances? Now the reality of this is that f a bigger portion of those who are lost are blacks and it is because more focus or time was needed to train and develop them. The other problem is that that three percent does not include the huge percentage of blacks that were not even hired or considered.

The other side to this is the black employees that work for large corporations and have to play the constant game of "How many black employees are there?" and then the next question is Why? So, if we are in need of more training or development based on the necessities of the job than we should. Because those that are looking for others like them in most cases fall into the three percent that is lost as well. I believe that is based on this easier to teach and work with mentality. Well no duh: we would like to report to people that look like us that share some sort of culture to lead us as well but that doesn't happen. If you are counting how many blacks work in your organization, then you are stifled by the amount in management! You as organizations have to take some accountability in that. If you are a coveted black employee (whatever that means) then you are very interested about what possibilities are available in the future and very proud of the organization they work for. Now three years goes by and that same employee is looking for another job because nothing has changed in the increase of black employees and especially in positions that someone is interested in. Your responsibility has to go farther than following specific guidelines from Washington DC. The tricky part says that even if we do get a black candidate we feel is worthy we may lose them because we have not taken the time to find more that are worthy.

## Try A Different Approach

There is a different approach when it comes to doing this with black and brown employees. We are used to sitting down and being told in some way that we are not good enough. I know that is not your fault but it is your approach that can change the game. We already know going in it will be a difficult conversation. Do not allow the power of making that decision to get in the way of the commitment you promised to the person you hired. If performance management is done the right way it seems as if it is a continued work in progress instead of a chase not to lose their job. Blacks are not as used to life in Corporate America as you are.

## Termination

Your paranoia around what might occur when terminating a black or brown person is the same issue our police have when they interact with them. They allow the stereotypes to dictate every interaction with them. This aggressive display that we see daily about what goes on in the ghetto does not mean that the interaction in your office will be the same. That aggressiveness was once about surviving the ghetto. Now it is about the passion for more so if you crush them or treat them as they have always been treated in their exit; it could diminish their ability to move forward. Do not allow yourself to think you have to be any more aggressive in your approach than you would with anyone else. Understand that the possibility of what is next diminishes with every opportunity even if the termination has to occur. Yeah, I get it you think that is a bit overdramatic. Tell that to the person that was finally able to provide for their family in a way they have and who now has to face the fact that things may be going back to the way they used to be, hoping they will get another opportunity. To you it is a short goodbye with a replacement ready to them it is another few years of losing opportunities just by walking in the door. They do not see this as a lost opportunity but a loss of a glimpse of what they thought life could be. I am just trying to paint a picture that looks more like panic and concern instead of aggressive and dangerous. In situations of termination circumstances our outlook does not have a light at the end of the tunnel. Learn from what you have seen or maybe a little from what you read here.

# COACHING

Coaching is at the behest of those who coach. The way to do it is directed by the organization or what plan they have put in place. If there is one way to coach all and get the same results that are based on company expectations please let the world know. You see certain folks from each class that seem to fall behind. Being honest about that is what is going to set us on the right path to allow those who coach to be true coaches. How many coaches go into the next season with the same exact coaching plan without understanding what the current problem is? Coaches in sports are able to curb the norm and adjust to the team players on the field but most of all realizing how to bring out the best in every player on the team. Corporations have failed in this regard.

Coaching is a very distinct function in all of business not just sales organizations. Every business has their concept of the perfect coaching strategy which always includes many strategies from other companies. Many succeed with this strategy to some extent but many fail. Then we move on to the next candidate. Are we even being honest enough to create a plan based on our failures as coaches or organizations so that we understand that the approach or continuous training has to be changed to fit each individual's level and ability? We invest and get locked into what we as an organization feel is the best way to coach and train our associates. The problem is we do not involve the reps being coached. We do not ask them what they think they need help with. This process puts a coach or trainer in a bind when trying to figure out how to make it work with those that are not assimilating the information they are being trained on. Think about the relationship that builds when you allow the associate to be a part of the process and the accountability they will achieve in the process.

The one thing that has always been mind-boggling to me is the quick acceptance of attrition. We have accepted this a part of the strategy which immediately suggests that not all will make it. Is this a sensible strategy? We want to believe that we did all we could for that associate, but we set expectations based on organizational wants that do not connect the dots with those we hire or our ability to be spontaneous in our approach to retain and continue growth of each person we hired. We wonder why in exit interviews a lot of people will talk about lack of coaching or support. On the other side we have those who do the training saying they coached them more than other associates. In the end the associate is right, because just because you did more of the training with the formality the business is looking for this does not necessarily mean it resonated with the associate you are training. If the coach and trainer have coached that associate more based on the data then they should be asking themselves if their coaching was impactful or just necessary without impact. We have accepted the law of averages and how we will lose a certain portion of the reps we hire but do not take into account that people are not pawns to play the corporate game with. These are people that trusted your organization would do all in their power to make that person successful. If you're willing to buy the fact that some will be lost no matter what and that you as an organization will not change your course of action or training then be honest up front so that help is sought out more often. To me this just reflects the old adage of "my way or the highway".

Have you ever walked by a room and see a fellow associate in a coaching sitting there with their heads down? This can result from one of two things maybe they do not like hearing their voice or maybe they do not get the concept as well in a 1:1 setting. Either way as organizations we use this as a checkbox activity for leaders, coaches or future leaders to say whether they are doing enough without asking them what is working so that we can continue to grow our team of those who coach and train.

The organization's concept of coaching may not coincide with the true need of the associate being trained. This concept is real across most organizations. Every coaching concept or lack thereof always starts with the organizations plight at a high level and is then passed down. They tell you how to coach then they tell you to change coaching or send you in a different direction based on the effect it has but still do not ask for your input even when it doesn't work. Think of a teacher they have to find a way to teach the content to each student. Yes, they have a curriculum that they are set to teach but if some fall behind they cannot just continue to teach straight through until others catch up. They have to adjust and find a way to bridge that gap and they have to find a way to keep those ahead of the game challenged. As with anything else some students will pick it up faster than others. They still have to find a way to make sure all students learn what is necessary to move to the next grade. My point is that they cannot just attrit certain kids in the class that do not meet the standards right away and just fail them because they would need to take part ownership in that as we all should do within our organizations. Some stay after class, some need extra help or tutoring. The bottom line is that it is the teacher's job to find a way to get through to each and every student. Our trainers and coaches should feel the same way. Forget expectations and stereotypes and if you know them it should give you even more ammunition to help others based on prior lost associates instead of continuing to move on to the next job hunter. Remember when these associates come in for jobs you are selling your organization as much as they are selling you on why they should be a part of it.

I know in most cases we are looking for the 1-2-3's and A-B-C's of coaching. How do you know what they are before we know who we are coaching? If you come up with the perfect strategy (I say hiding my smile as I do) do we consider that the strategy might not be perfect for all, or do we accept that if it is not perfect for all that they are not the right fit for the organization? That is the standstill or crossroad between success of many or success of specific associates. Coaching needs to be about dissecting the strengths and opportunities of each rep and finding out how you can "unleash talent"! Sit down with the rep and ask the question Why? Every person matters because you are a team trying to complete a mission TOGETHER regardless of your rank or title. The first step to good coaching is the buy-in of those being coached. How many times at a senior level of management do we ask our reps how they feel the coaching is going, instead of just relying on a get it or get out mentality? Thinking one size fits all for all associates we coach is our biggest mistake; not setting up one way to coach or one style makes your possibilities endless. If they feel they are part of the process they want to be a part of the solution as well. Understand that I am not saying that the principles steps and guidelines in other books or organizations do not work but I would say if you asked five associates one of those five would say it does not work for them. Then think about the cost to train and hire and how twenty percent of your hires are just fodder for attrition, because of the inflexible and unresponsive approach to coaching and development.

## Group Coaching

Group coaching is an amazing opportunity to share ideas and that should be the true focus of organizations. Do not be afraid to allow those closest to it to be a part of the plan we come up with otherwise we are just guessing. It is easy to see in these meetings which associates are comfortable with the content or training. There is a great chance that they are writing notes but are they internalizing the information? Will it make sense to them when they go back to read the notes? It is difficult to assess this. In fact, a lot of times if there is a presentation with slides, they are literally writing down exactly what they see on the screen. Is that effective? I guess it depends on the person and how sticky the information being coached or trained to is. Will it help build sustainable performance? Whenever something becomes a task it is no longer a learning. Our recognition of this as trainers, coaches, leaders and as organizations need to make sure that all are moving along in the process. If not, you continue to run into staggered performances across all of your associates. I am a believer that retraining is better than hiring new associates. Retraining reps to play catch up because you did not recognize they were falling behind in previous training is counterproductive if we do not own our part in that and just put the pressure on them to perform at a higher level.

Sit down with those reps and remember if you take the time to know them, the signs become clearer. Hint hint, get to know the people that you are asking daily to leave it all out there for you and the organization. Ask them if they understand the information and direction. We tend to think calling on the person that does not seem engaged is the go-to option. I can tell you by experience that one of two things will happen. Either they will read back to you what they copied from the presentation or two. They will shut down even more which will stifle their engagement altogether. Ask yourself if that happens across four percent of your business on the norm how much does that skew the P & L for your business. While the data and analytics will tell part of the story it will never tell the execs how impactful your efforts were or what part of what you were doing with those lost associates did not work. We are not getting in front of it when it's all about the data. Instead, we are letting the data make the decision in the long run for that associate. By then, their ability to rebound or mentally they are already checked out based on what the data didn't tell us but if we knew our reps, we could tell by the look on their face daily. Organizations become comfortable pulling those associates out of the analytics at that point, because we have already chalked them up as a loss to the business or that they are incapable of doing the job.

## Are Blacks Really Coached?

Now close your eyes and think about the same circumstances but it is a black candidate. I wanted to start with the approach used in general by most corporations regardless of color or creed before I enlightened you on how that obviously impacts blacks more than their white counterparts. Our ability to learn and catch on is not about basic abilities. It is more about having the resources necessary. The simplicity of asking about how proficient they are in Word, Excel, PowerPoint, etc. is not as easy to answer for black associates. Some do not even have a computer or a laptop. So, if it entails what they teach in school it will help to some degree but the capability to grab the laptop and build a spreadsheet is like speaking a different language to us. We should always coach with the openness that one size does not fit all. We have to be deliberate in our approach to make sure that all are on board as you move through the training.

# Get To Know
# Our Culture

---

## Dress Code

This is always a tricky one and not as a black and white issue as it often assumed to be. People in sweat suits can be just as successful as those in business suits. This should be an easy one because corporations can basically set their dress code rules any way they want to. Those rules may even get lenient. There are two parts to this that need to be focused on. We have different cultures so you should expect different styles. I am not talking about the obnoxious fad of your pants hanging off your ass. I mean different does not mean better or worse it just means that if we get to understand each other's cultures we would stop turning our noses up to at each other's beliefs. What is the difference if you wear a two-piece suit, and someone else wears jeans and sneakers with a button-down and tie? Who actually stated that the two-piece looked better? Maybe we should just put a picture in the code of conduct book with no words and dress exactly like the person in the picture? Our differences are what make so many others indulge in our American ways. They are not just interested in coming from other countries because of the guy they saw in the suit. The sad part is that their freedoms and opportunities make more sense than what blacks are accustomed to.

Another factor that plays a role is affordability! Many who see that two-piece suit would love to put it on but cannot afford the tie that goes with it, let alone the suit. Even in interviews be careful not to judge someone walking in the door without a suit on. I love to hear people say things like, "Well, you can go to a place where people donate clothes and get a suit". First of all, that will give the white employees one more thing to make fun of; the other is they may have already gone there to get the jeans and dress shirt to wear for the interview. Again it's the simple explanation or the understanding that you should be dressed a certain way which again puts us at a disadvantage. Maybe they can buy some suits if they get opportunities to do so. They may feel uncomfortable with their only option to wear and have to see everyone else they are competing with for the job in suits in the lobby.

Make up is different for women in different cultures. Hair styles are different in different cultures. The fact that we had to pass legislature so that people could not be discriminated against for their hair style is a pure example of bullshitting your way past a problem. This was about dreadlocks, cornrows, etc. I want you to stop right here for a second as a white person and think about what your first response was or would be if you saw a man or woman with dreads or cornrows. It's ok it's not just you because these are the simple thoughts that continue to get tossed around. What that is telling black people is that we have to change who we are and our appearance just to be in a position to get a job? If we are being honest some executives feel like it may scare customers. Here is the thing just because you put something in place that says a company cannot discriminate based on hair style you're just giving them something else to pay attention to. There may not be a question on the sheet about hair or the ability to address it but their reaction and feelings about it will not change come decision time. You cannot tell us we didn't get the job because of the fact that we are black either but it is obvious based on the lopsided approach by corporations.

Gold chains or bulky chains do not identify people as drug dealers or rappers. That is something white society came up with so that their negligence goes unnoticed. I heard President Obama say one time that people should stop buying the Jordans or gold chains and save for a car or other "meaningful" things. I love Barrack, but that comment is one from a Harvard grad. You see hood mentality is the ability to buy those Jordans or that first gold chain that everyone on the block already had. That was our Mercedes because if you visit one of those lots and you're black you will probably feel the same as you do in the boardroom ALONE. I do not think black people think about things like building a foundation for their family, buying a car, or buying a house. You cannot make statements like that unless you have been there. Ask how long it took to save up for those Jordans or that gold chain then tell me how long it would take for them to have enough to even walk past the

Mercedes dealership and feel good. It is our way of feeling good about buying something that we could afford and call our own. My true answer to my idol would be if you grow up in a neighborhood where a lot of people have nice chains your first chain is an accomplishment you couldn't believe. If you grow up in a neighborhood where the bills are paid and life is better well it makes sense that your goal is the new house or retirement fund. You cannot change the hood or the perspective by telling us what we should do without money. We have to build programs that allow these things that seem out of reach for black men and women, and give them the opportunity to learn how to invest their money, how to understand how short money feels good but long money is part of how you leave a legacy and foundation for your family. If you stand on the block and say "Here is a job that will help take care of your families" the sneaker store or jewelry store won't seem like such a huge accomplishment. It is the accomplishment to gain or have something you never had before. Those accomplishments regardless of how they seem to others are a glimpse of hope that more is possible.

## Pronunciation

This is high on the list because I have heard it more times than I can count. It relates to our ideas of what is and what isn't perfect language. If a person is Hispanic and learns English we give them credit for being bilingual and sometimes pay more for that reason. It doesn't matter how broken some of the English words are as long as they have the ability to communicate. If a black person says "worf" instead of "worth however, it is assumed that he can no longer do the job at the same level as others. This again is a very blatant falsity that we deal with on a regular basis. How does using an "f" instead of a"th" at the end of a word and using "the correct pronunciation" change the vernacular of where the conversation is going or point that is made? Do you know that some black people think it is funny that white people over-enunciate? The worst part is that as many times as I have heard it. I still have never heard that white leader address the person saying it which means it is not as important as you think. It also means there is no rule in the hiring handbook that said you have to pronounce words a specific way to do this job.

Maybe we should go back to the teachers that we had going through school and persecute them for allowing a little of our culture to show through as we moved grade to grade. I look at is it as another stereotype not to include certain people. Now we do not look like you or talk like you meaning we are already on two strikes. Our only in hope is that it it is like baseball and we get one more. This at times is proof that people are aware of differences but they would rather point them out or make fun of something they do not understand. If we changed the meaning of the word or used it in a way where it eludes the true meaning of the word such discrimination would make more sense. But this is not the case: it is just but because we say it differently than most of YOU know that it is wrong or worthy of ridicule.

So, what you're saying is we talk different; what I am saying is that we walk different, talk different, dress different, listen to different music and watch different movies. That is culture and whether we want to learn from that culture or not it is not going away. Our path is just anemic based on your efforts to even the playing field. I wanted to bring some light to this since it is not talked about but it is deemed necessary to say in front of a black man you presume to be more educated because he found a way to sound more vanilla when he or she speaks. We pronounce words different than others that are the same color as us, and vice versa. Some people understand that some of our words are from other countries and they are not spoken exactly the same, but we took the Latin or French root of a word and made it our own. If you are ever confused when speaking to a black person know that this is all we really have done: changed the word to better fit our liking or the way the masses say it. The only word that is the same in both is fair whether we want to own that or not.

# Black Music

Our music is a revolution of how tough life can be. There are no punches pulled on making sure our stories and culture are understood everywhere. Just because you hear a few lyrics that are misunderstood or that you think are raw does not make it a lie.

"Rap music" is what I hear our music referred to. It allows those who are not as interested in our music to defy it. Saying you do not like to hear the music just explains to us why you do not want to get to know us as well. You tie rap music to violence and drugs. All we grew up around was violence and drugs. It is an excuse not to listen to the truth about what is going on in the ghettos that we grew up in. White folks sing about hope and rainbows. We wake up to gun-fire and crowds on the corner selling dime bags.

It is a pure revelation that not liking a specific genre of music is ok but if you're trying to silence people that have generally been silenced forever by not at least listening to the lyrics, this is a different matter. You label it as rap, we label it as hip hop. Rap gives you a word to dissect or a way to persecute those for their beliefs and experiences.

Hip hop is what we use. Rap is just a word, but hip hop is LOVE. It was something we could call our own and have the ability to celebrate our culture. A way for us to tell stories that some are afraid to hear. The words used are hard but so was life. If you take a minute to internalize it you will understand that these black men and women that are never heard found an avenue to tell our stories to the world. If it is that bad then why are there white rappers as well? Why has our culture become so attracted to it? Listening to our music and wearing our clothes has become a must. The problem is you're not listening to what we are saying. The only culture of music that is heard where you will hear undeniable truth about the differences that keep us apart is ours. If you walk into a business it is definitely not in the elevator music file. We need to be careful if we play music in the office because it is more aggressive but you hear it on many commercials on TV. The world is changing and corporations are lagging behind. Your goal is not to find that happy medium for all. It's about going with the status quo. Where there is a minimal amount of black people in the company, it makes it even harder. How does that person become more relevant within the business when they cannot talk to anyone else about their culture or favorite music because people will consider them to be beneath them, like they always have?

# Role Models

Who do you consider role models in your organizations and what do those role models look like? This is a role where the more you have or the more you have access to is the difference maker in corporations. Hope is built around watching others that look like you succeed that look like you. It is about better role models than we have known. When this happens, we start believing there is a life outside of the hood. Our plight changes, our beliefs change and our passion for begins to outweigh the destruction that has occurred up to this point.

I have had some great role models in my career and most of them were white and great people to their core. I still didn't see any that looked like me and I always wondered why it wasn't such a big deal to everyone else. Ask yourself when a team member, leader or executive walks into a room how comfortable do they feel? At first you just think you are the first and you want to believe that before you question or challenge the status quo. Then you start to question why there are no more coming. Then you question how much you are really wanted or accepted within that organization. Then you think about whether it is a long-term job or whether other opportunities will one day be available to you.

In all of this the toughest part of this delineation we go through trying to find our place is accepting this treatment. Alternatively the "hood thinking" kicks in where you try to be happy that you got out. Should I say anything or just be happy I have a job? To us it is like being offered a plea deal but with no intention to help anyone else. There is an understanding about prison and most of its occupants being of minority descent. Another understanding is that most corporations are filled with more white than other ethnic backgrounds. So, think about going to jail as a white person and all the fears that come with that. That is how blacks feel when they walk into a corporate office where no one looks like them.

We need strong role models to see what we have not our whole lives. That is a lot to ask but not hard to do. Remember, many of us did not have a father growing up or others around us that were not good examples but were rather trying to live in the lap of luxury in the hood. Our chance to learn more and get a better feel on what is necessary to do it will come from role models some will have to be white, black, hispanic along with other ethnicities.

My message for other blacks that have made it is that it is our responsibility to change the end of this story. We have to be bold enough to speak out and ask the tough questions that no one wants to answer. As I said earlier, I get the feeling of "how will I find anything else?" but we have to be confident about what we have proven or that we are as capable or even more capable to be role models. I do not mean to scream out loud on the floor about the inadequacy of how the business is being run. Should we run to HR? How do you fight fear with fire?

Use the opportunities you are given to uplift your people. We still want to think about the business and the expectations they are looking for but we have to get away from thinking that will only happen at its best with white people at the helm. Some of them have been doing it for so long that we do not question it but our actions and ability to work within a system that doesn't seem to want us there. We have to be humble in our achievements so they seem possible to those that look like us but we also have to be honest in our conversations about how hard it will be. Make sure they understand what the corporate world is not by focusing on the impact we can have on it in the future.

We have to find ways to connect with our neighborhoods so that we can start to transform what black neighborhoods, black people and black opportunities look like. This is the only way things will change. Believing you can change the norm is hard but we owe it to those we love and those who look like us. We have gone generations already and this is the difference in when they say we are making excuses. Realizing that at some point and doing something to promote the possibilities for blacks win, lose or draw it is hard to call that an excuse. If you have a family where one after the other passes down the same reason for things not getting better then yes it becomes an excuse.

Partners to work with and a buddy system is something I have seen used to build up the support systems for employees. The problem here is that if executives in these organizations do not understand how to lead or promote black men how would a peer that sits right next to them, that look exactly like the executives in the business help? It's just an ongoing process of tweaking the original process a little or looking for a little more consistency in how they support and train their reps. My analogy to this would be the same as bowling a ball down the alley hoping you hit at least one pin then jumping for joy when that one pin falls. Bring in some experienced black associates from other businesses to get their input on what it will take to change the current and persisting issues around diversity and inclusion. You can bring them in as consultants to the business so that their honesty is what you get and what you should really want.

Then you have business partners who come to visit the business. These groups show up looking the exact same as those you see going into the conference rooms at work. Now you have a situation where your idea that there could be more diversity within other organizations is shattered. It starts to feel like a jail no one can escape from. How about a party that you will never be invited to? Maybe just walking down the street to look at houses you can never buy. While exaggerated this is the conundrum that we have to work through daily about the real world and what it has to offer. You can continue to stand on the sidelines hoping someone else takes the risk or you could be the game changers that change business and opportunities as we know them today.

## Get to Know Their Families

Culture is better understood when you see families together. You see the love and joy we find in each other and how open we are to those who are genuine. You understand how some of us get through the tragedies of the ghetto and with nothing we have more love in our hearts than we will ever get credit for. The paranoia you think you see. The defense mechanism that you think we always have up. The aggression or violent nature portrayed for blacks. The few extra questions that you think we ask based on lack of trust. All of these things will be better understood in the element of families. Honestly it will help with your comfort around us or your tentative approach at hiring us as well. You truly see the element when we are with our families that let us all know that they are like us. We work hard for and love our loved ones. It is a way for you to meet more of us and find the comfort in the celebration of life even if it does not look as good to us as everyone else. It can also show you the difference in how happy that black associate could be if he had more like him in the business.

# Phrases to Stay Away from in The Workplace

## You All

This infers that you consider us different. It also takes a persona and stereotype that we are all alike. If we walked around saying "you all" it would make sense because you are the majority but it would still be something frowned upon. You have to sharpen yourselves with knowledge because the first time you make the mistake of saying something you have heard or that you deem ok from a limited perspective we believe that is who you are forever. You are completely disregarding the trust that was built with that employee.

## You're Not Like the Others

Most will throw this out in conversation and consider it a compliment. We should be proud because we know the truth to why we are like the others, why we stand with the others and knowing that the others may have just had a tougher ride or fewer avenues out. Your intent is to make

---

49

one black man or woman feel better by saying they are better than other black people. Why would we feel better about the fact that you have just made us king or queen of all that is black? You say "you are not like them" and we hear your meaning as I'm so glad you are not violent and scary. In all honesty everyone you meet should be different. If we had to live in a world of categorizing who we work with, it would be a few of us and a lot of them. We would not tell you that you are different from the others because the others have always treated us the same and at some point, the treatment means more than the relation to what we want people to be. Maybe we should focus on diversifying our thoughts and plans so that we expand the ability to grow our businesses. Please if this is something you have ever said think about this: What if the others are just like the one you think you are complimenting but you never gave them a chance to prove to be just as good?

## You Look Like So and So from That (Movie or Show)

This is another primal approach at trying to find a way to communicate with someone. To us it is another way to say we all look alike. Some of these will fall heavily into this category. Again, there are just as many lookalikes for white men and women as well. The difference is there are a lot fewer black entertainers and actors so it expounds the impression it has on blacks when you say it. Maybe it is a compliment but why is it that we do not have to find your doppelganger to have a conversation? You find things to relate us to as if we are foreign or different than you. In reality no one wants to believe they look exactly like someone else anyway so imagine how the other person feels when you have to yell out the name of an actor or someone in entertainment to give us the proper greeting.

## I Get Scared When I Get Pulled Over Too

These are tough situations because you may have been pulled over and you may have been scared. It is hard for us to believe that you do not see the difference in how blacks and whites are treated. So, our look isn't based on the fact that we do not believe you. It is that you are trying to compare what happens to us every day to something that may have happened once to you or your dad on a drive home one day.

The other important thing is that you are not scared for your life. You are scared of getting points on your license or how mad your mom and dad will be that you got pulled over in their car. We are worried that they are going to cause us harm. That is not a thought it is a reality based on what we still see every day. Think about having a conversation with a woman that lost a child. Our empathy needs to be about that person and that situation so you letting them know the same thing happened to you too does not help the conversation it just turns the attention to you. It is ok to be vulnerable in conversations when it is warranted, but when you are trying to justify ongoing flat out corruption by the police based on a one off situation when you got pulled over then to us it seems like you are trying to fit our centuries worth of pain into a small envelope.

## I Was Poor Growing Up Too

This can be the truth for a lot of people but before even going here think about your situation and what you know about most blacks. What did your poor look like? It probably looked like the kid a few blocks away that had a nicer house or car. For us it was you that's right the white people that say we were poor growing up were the ones we envied because they had a ton more than we did. We are not questioning what you think poor is we are just extremely sure that it is not the poor that we encountered. Things like a Christmas tree with no presents under it not getting a car when we are seventeen instead of sixteen.

You also have to remember that as decades go on and generations churn we have seen even worse which makes the so-called "I was poor too" comment even less rational. Poor does not equal poor. Growing up black gives a different and more profound meaning to things like poor that even our ancestors could equate to. There are other nationalities that were treated horribly in the past but our treatment has always been there and continues to this day. When is our pause? When can our poor be the same poor you think it is? The next time that statement seems like the right one do me a favor and sit down with the black person and see if you poor matches their understanding of it growing up.

# All Lives Matter, Not Just Blacks Lives

This is a true statement. The problem black people have with it is that you only say it when we say Black Lives Matter. It is your retort to try to establish that our saying "Black Lives Matter" implies that we don't feel that all lives matter. When your unemployment rate is equal to ours, the rate of murders by police, education opportunities. I could go on and on then sure, equivalent action would be justified. You see when you continue to realize that the horrible things can still happen in broad daylight you say it because you need to believe it. We need to believe that our black youth will not be crucified as they get older just for being black. When we say black lives matter, we do not mean that white lives do not. When you say all lives matter not just BLACKS it means that you think we matter even less.

We have all the reasons you do not to say black lives matter. We have the pain and anguish, the loss and hurt, the incarceration and the plan to keep incarcerating. When whites become more concerned with why we are saying it and more honest and vocal with the fact that if all lives matter whites and blacks would not live so differently well then, we have a chance to hold hands and say together ALL LIVES MATTER! Until that becomes a reality do not fight back with statements that black people can poke holes in because the irony in that statement is just like every other one. Everyone knows they just do not want to be the first to say so. If you acknowledge that you truly get it, we would not measure the gap between the two races we would listen because you did.

## We Are All Discriminated Against

This one should go without saying but unfortunately too many times it does not. It is hard for me to say as I did in the prior suggestion that there is some truth to this. When discriminated becomes part of the rebuttal the gap is so huge it is not even worth trying to justify the statement if it is not a black or brown person saying it. That word has been ingrained in the business world mainly around the treatment of blacks. There are some great other additions beyond color that are powerful as well, but the reality is that when people see the word discrimination they see black people. It is ok for that comparison to happen but then understand that thinking that one black man got a job over a white man does not qualify as discrimination when you look around and see the lack of diversity within your own office.

## Are You All Black (Meaning Mixed)?

This is definitely NO GOOD. I am black and white so I have experienced this my whole life. You know how to make a mixed black person feel even worse. Ask them that question. It seems as if it is an interrogation and you are picking your poison. Now I always say my mother is white because she raised me on her own and regardless of how people see me that is a white woman that deserves her due! If we are not mixed and just a light-skinned black person, it is even more offensive because then the question becomes, "Why does that even matter?". If they are a little lighter does that mean you are more comfortable because they look a little whiter? It immediately gives us the clear ability to see that it matters to you. It doesn't matter because you are truly interested in our lineage or who we are. It is a way for you to amplify the comfort and in your minds thinking that if they look a little different the label may not have to be the same. Well here is the simple answer to that. It does not matter if you are all black, light-skinned, multi-racial; we are black. There is no shade that is considered any differently unless it is a white person trying to wrap their heads around what the best option is. We are all quite all right if you call us black or should I say "African American".

## Do You Play Sports?

This one is important for a few reasons. Growing up sports was one of the only things we thought could get us out of the ghetto. So first off yes, many blacks you meet were probably very good at or played sports. Sometimes they become great players but still did not get to the big dance. You think we all think we are going to the NFL or NBA. Most of our parents gave the last that they had for us to be able to join teams. They did this with the hope that if nothing else it could earn them a scholarship to college that would allow them better opportunities than they had.

It is not the question that bothers us. It is your assumption that disturbs most. Remember these young men and women are trying to find a better life. Some of them did have dreams of going to college or the pros and never had the opportunity. The last thing they want to do is start a conversation with the old "so do you play sports" reminder.

If there are corporations that have leagues and teams within the organization, then treat it as you do most things post a notice about it so that it can be seen by anyone. Then if someone of color wants to play they do not feel stereotyped by your ask. Well actually it would be different because I am sure that in most larger companies your posting for a C-level position would be less likely for a black candidate then playing power forward on the corporate basketball team. We already know that you have succumbed to the idea that we are more athletic than others. If it is the only conversation that lights up your eyes when looking at that black candidate then they might as well go back to the courts in the ghetto with no nets and take their chances.

## My Family Started with Nothing

This is very true, but in most cases, these are groups that are deserving of that conversation and some very tough times. With all due respect to all of those our stories go for centuries and still have not let up. I actually know families that started with nothing and finished with nothing. The average person that truly understands what nothing feels like would never bring it up in conversation themselves. They would carry strength and hard learnings from it but there is always that embarrassment of how hard things were for our families financially. You say this to us to try to break the ice and help us feel better about what we went through. How many times does the black person bring it up in convo? Even if they do there are levels to everything so you cannot compare based on what your ancestors went through and find commonality in what we go through and our ancestors that went through worse. Your knowledge of the worst time for your nationality come a dime a dozen for black men and women in this country then and now. You do not have to set the stage or even the playing field by making us feel better about our poverty by trying to compare it to yours. It just helps us continue to revisit how bad things were for us and the fact that you may never truly understand that.

## Why Do There Need to Be Diversity Groups? What About White People?

There is not a whole lot to explain here. A question like this is another reason for the adage white privilege. My answer for anyone that would actually bring themselves to ask that question would be: Look around and look how diverse your team is not even the whole company just your area then ask yourself why there needs to be diversity groups. The answer is simple. Look around your neighborhoods, look around your companies, look around the schools your kids attend, do the research to see why and then applaud this effort from companies that are willing to do it.

## Insinuating a Black Associate Is Friends with Another Black Associate

This is a common mistake in the workplace that can be avoided easily. It is visible with the ease of just lifting your head and looking around. Okay, so you're in the leader meeting and all of the leaders are white except you. We do not think based on the fact that you seem chummy with the others in there that you are friends. Maybe you have worked together for a long time or maybe it is simply because you have more in common. Now think about that over an entire organization. We tend to find each other and have conversations as well but maybe it is just simply because we have more in common. The reason this happens is because there are so few of us that if you see us talk a few different times or each lunch together we are friends. The only difference is if we insinuated that you were all friends based on a few conversations going on; it would just make it even lonelier for us.

## Prettiest Black Girl or Most Handsome Black Man I Have Ever Seen

Versus? The extreme to this is that it makes you come off as if you have never seen one before. I am not talking about seeing pretty black women or handsome black men.

I mean seeing a black person! I get it that seems farfetched, but if you say that does it mean, not as pretty as a white woman or as handsome as a white man? Do not try to justify our beautiful queens and kings by using black in front of what you actually think is a compliment.

## What Do You Think About the First Black Person That Did That? (Presidency, Entertainment, Etc.)

Another unthoughtful comment or question. What if the response was what do you think about it? It is our attempt at times to be supportive but that still does not entail the research or the empathy that needs to be understood before wanting us to be excited about situations like this. What do I think? I think it is a shame that it took forty-three others before a black man became president. Think about the fact that we are in 2020 and we are still saying this. I wonder if you understand what it feels like to have to wait centuries after others to get a portion of what whites have and still be mountains from equality. Please stop thinking it is a big deal for a black person to do something for the first time when you know it has been done by many others and start to educate yourself on why it took so long. Most of us know that if we had the opportunity it would have happened a long time ago. This will help you understand that what seems like a compliment is travesty.

# I Love Rap Music

First of all, those who love our music call it hip hop. Rap music or rappers is a name others gave it to further stereotype our people or to have a reason to tell their white sons and daughters that they cannot play it in the house anymore. "That damn rap music".

Hip hop is love! It is our celebration of life or lack thereof. It is our best stories and our worst. It is our voice that we were able to display without your permission to do so. Hip hop was something we did with a broken-down radio tapping on a forty bottle with a quarter or someone pounding on the hood of the closest car. It was our way to celebrate our brilliance while you try to deny us that if there are certain songs you do not like. That is the whole purpose! You have to read deeper into the lyrics to understand the PAIN behind them. You may not always like them but when no one hears you most of the time; we want to make sure that when they do they truly get it. If you really love it then do not just dance to the music listen to the words and you will fall in love with it so much more.

# So Do Black People

This is another easy mistake to make and another statement usually made purely on the misunderstanding of white privilege. We say that as a compliment giving you the benefit of the doubt by saying you just didn't know. We go along with it even if we do believe it is obvious to see the standard set. When you respond to others commenting on what some have whether it be resources, jobs or other opportunities and you respond, "So do black people," we should immediately have the right to say "How much less?" Just because you see some it doesn't mean that the floodgates opened. It just means that you think they are open enough and that is all we deserve for right now.

## Things Have Gotten a Lot Better

If you are speaking to a black person or around one try to stay away from this. It sounds like you feel bitter because it has gotten better for them. It also makes it seem as if you are content with the landslide that is visible in every situation that compares blacks and whites. The next question they will have is compared to what? Your visibility, want or need to investigate and research the truth to all of this is how you can answer your own question. Are you talking about the slavery days? The hypocrisy around this states to us you are uneducated, fail to understand or simply blind to the reality of what you look around and see. We are not asking you to write a dissertation on it, we just want you to again acknowledge the disparities before you try to shore up the efforts or really the lack thereof to build a united diverse front.

## That Is So Ghetto

This is one heard weekly by most black people. Some say it thinking that we can relate to it which is obnoxious so we will remove them from this conversation. If you are saying this to a black person and the situation you are explaining is "ghetto" worthy. that tells us a few things. You think the ghetto is a terrible place or that anyone who acts "ghetto" is considered less worthy than others. You are right about one thing, it is a terrible place to have to grow up but what is even more terrible is that you have no idea what it's like and you are saying it in front of someone that grew up there. The worst part is, if you are honest about where you grew up with that employee or leader. Think about the worst stereotype or label you give a person being based on the fact that they grew up poor and where you grew up was called the ghetto. Every time we look at you whether you are misunderstood or not we will remember the word and the look on your face when you said it!

## I Do Not See Color

This is a clear relation to the term colorblindness which is another adjective used often. You think by saying this that it will in some way disregard how we feel about the fact that you even needed to say it. It is also a sell-out way to solidify our thoughts based on your action. It is a way for some white people to hide from racism or the ability to get involved.

Read this closely: WE NEED YOU TO SEE COLOR! You do not see us that is the problem. We need you to truly see us so that you will not be scared, intimidated, defensive or so that you can get to know us and the stereotypes will no longer rule the hiring world. The better part is you will have a better understanding of why these impulses you have when you are around us are unnecessary. You will see us as equals if you see us. You will realize you do have a whole lot more than most black people you even know and let's be honest, how many do you ACTUALLY know? We continue to show great strengths apart. Imagine what we could do together!

## Oh, Your Husband or Wife Is Black?

This is just a no-no! Remember in most cases if the significant other is there, it is a party or some sort of beverage filled night. This is where black people feel the most uncomfortable because it is when white folks are most honest. This question is not even close to what you hear from the "good ole boys" or the "mean girls" at a work happy hour. It can change your relationship with that person forever. It is not just the mistake of being surprised by the fact that mixed couples exist it's the fact that it mattered.

Remember this is the person they love as much as the person you love regardless of color. Because love is love right? Everyone believes that! Then why does it matter what color the people are that are in love?

## I Have Black Friends

Ummm we do too? I would bet my savings that our black friends probably never met. They also probably did not grow up in the same area. Knowing a few black people does not give you the ability to join into a conversation or pass judgment for that matter on black people or a black person. Why do you expect us to be exactly alike? Are you exactly like your white co-workers? Your justification for why you think it is ok to comment does not equal our pain and history that you decided to neglect all these years! There is no way to consume enough from a few friends that would educate you about all black people. Even if you are using it to comfort someone else just say sorry because you would not say that to anyone else in the same situation. Do not try to be empathetic to the point of needing to justify it. If you are paying attention to it and acknowledging the fact that it is not right and speaking out when necessary well, then you might end up with one more black friend.

# Words Matter:

---

**Accountability:** This is a tricky word. When you talk to accountability make sure you accept your part in that. If a black person gets a job but doesn't feel like they got the proper training or development they will make it known. You leave the door open by not making sure your training and development programs are not designed for the "already prepared". Why is it that you do not address this until they are failing or struggling? It becomes a tool in their eyes to naturally let those go who are not performing. How many people in your organization make the comeback necessary to enjoy a career? How many of them are black? Over the years I heard a lot of talk around how it was working based on attracting the right people. Maybe the true question is do we have the right people developing. Leaders are not trainers so they tend to take struggle personally. When that person struggles, they should take it personally but not pushing the blame back to the rep when your commitment to them originally is to lead through the good times and bad. Blacks expect a different type of accountability so when you tell them they are not being accountable have something to back that up with. Do a little homework before the conversation. Make sure you have the data to prove what the current situation is and a solid plan of how to turn things around. This should not just involve what is expected by the black associate but also what part the leader will play in that process.

Accountability to black people means helping raise your younger brother or sister. It means making sure you survive in the neighborhood you grew up in just to have an opportunity for a better life. It means taking care of your parents or working low-end jobs to help pay bills at a very young age. It means accepting what we can get because of who we are or how we look and still working as hard as possible to get a step ahead. It means you grew up in a tough neighborhood and still had to find a way not to be around the toughest parts of the ghetto. Accountability meant trying to do what others in the hood were not and the responsibility of being the first in the family or in your hood to go to college or get a good job. It means looking out for family and friends in the hood that cannot look out for themselves. Accountability for us is about staying alive long enough to succeed or fail. It is about walking past all the devilish ways of the hood so that you get a good job at some point. Accountability is about running into police officers and not getting killed, or not getting caught because a record for a black man is already a sentence. It is hard enough not to be judged just walking in the door with a record a black man or woman becomes just a statistic.

**Conspiracy Theory:** This one is tricky and used a lot

in corporate conversations. This is a theory in the world of discrimination that is used all the time. If you think they are asking too many questions, if they want a better explanation and for goodness sake if you want black people to stop thinking that way then hire some more that look like them. I ask if you constantly walked into a building where you didn't see many in the position you are in and even fewer in the positions that we may aspire to then isn't that the pure definition to what looks like a conspiracy theory? We have to ask ourselves a question every day that we cannot say out loud. Why are there so few of us here or "WHERE ARE ALL OF THE BLACK PEOPLE AT". We want to believe there is an explanation for it. Our inability to ask or vouch for our brethren makes us feel bad about our success. We worry if we become curious enough to ask then the ratio of white to black in the office may become one less.

Here is the question to the white leaders or HR specialists why are there so few blacks in your organization? How do you answer it? You flood us with mini cultural events, tell us about your diversity efforts (most of which are government-mandated) and point out the one black leader in the business who probably outdid all expectations just to get the job. If we take a minute to listen to them openly we will find out that every day that same black leader comes to work surmounted with the pressure of outworking his counterparts just to stay in that role. It is a simple question.

Why do you have such a staggering difference in the diversity of your employees and what have you done to change that? Ask that at your next big wig meeting and watch how everyone else freezes or looks as if they want to crawl in the corner but the one black guy can finally smile about what he has frowned about for the entire duration of his tenure with the company. I am trying to explain this in a different way because my definitions of these words and the impact that they can have are different than what you will see when you look them up in the dictionary. When our normal conversations are all the same, we forget that to some certain words in certain situations are a lot more harmful than they are to others. Part of this is not their fault because white privilege isn't explained to those who have it. That would not make sense and it is easier to see its ghost than to believe that another race does not have the same opportunities because they are black. This conversation around what you say and who you say it to is only relevant because of the disparity in how many have the conversations that are white to the lopsided whiteness of those they are having conversations with. Maybe if we hired more blacks those having the conversations would get better call it more practice!

What you're really asking when you say "This is not a conspiracy theory" is not to believe all the years we have seen the deck stacked against us or the data and statistics that prove we are on the bottom of the totem pole. You are asking us not to look around in the business we work in and get concerned about future opportunities based on who we are when you cannot prove we are wrong based on what you are currently doing. You're asking us to believe that everything the world proves true in that moment of conversation is no longer true because it is not your intent.

Our intent has to be researched and confirmed before we can make sense of it. Just because we know the intent isn't there you should still be aware enough of your team or team players to understand why we take some things more personal than others. To you we are too sensitive and taking it personal, or the infamous answer "I didn't mean it that way" or "I am sorry if you took it that way".

When we hear "conspiracy theory" we think differently. Did you say the same thing to the white candidates because of what you think is us being paranoid? We feel like it downplays the efforts it took to get to the point where we can be looked at as equals. We have been told our whole lives the world is against us so you are defying all of those with good reason to think so going back decades. When we hear it, we wonder if you even know why you are saying it. Again, the toughest part for black men and women is not playing catch up based on our lost opportunities it is that you will not acknowledge that the road for blacks is not harder than the road they paved for you. Companies put themselves in the position that the government allows so that they can say they are strong around diversity and culture but along the same lines as anyone else. You cannot use race in your decisions but it doesn't mean you still cannot make a decision based on race. You think if you have a problem with our dialect or pronunciation that isn't a form of discrimination because you made up some other standard reason for them not being the choice. When you say conspiracy theory we feel bad because the number one1 rule for a black man or woman is not to wonder why the discrepancy is there, but to be happy we got a chance regardless of how many didn't get one. When you say these things to us, it is a blatant disregard of our history and reality. If you cannot prove there isn't by the standards set by your organization or the environment that does not justify than there isn't a conspiracy theory hiring or retaining blacks over whites than do not go there. Conversations had for the sake of the associate and not the business should not include implications that they feel they are being singled out. We look around and see that there already are not many of us then when we are singled out and unspoken words are said, it does seem like it looks. Think about trying to get someone to believe in something they have never experienced before but treating them the same as they have always been treated.

**Selfish:** I believe those who are selfish either never had to share or do not realize what it is like to want the things that most people need. Selfish is about having something you do not want to share so to the average black person the selfish approach is to hire the easy agent or those that fit the profile. If you come from nothing your idea of selfish was taking one more serving before others got to eat not just because that is contrary to basic dinner etiquette, but for us because we have to make sure there is enough to go around for all. You say selfish because we are asking for more when you have no clue how long it has been since we have not had anything or that as black people we are still trying to figure out if we actually have anything to be selfish with.

Selfish in a black neighborhood can be who you left behind or who the hood has taken. We feel bad at times because we have made it but saw a lot who didn't or probably never will. We feel selfish for having a nice car when others from the hood are still on the bus or looking for a ride or because we move to another neighborhood and left behind everyone we knew. My point here is black people blame themselves for doing better at times because others cannot but those who employ us do not see the selfishness in giving more opportunities to those who look like them, or who went to the same alma mater.

There is a deeper meaning to every word we say and unfortunately that expands even more from one culture to another. We allow others to live off our freedoms and sometimes never learn the language at all but their skill sets and abilities somehow bring about jobs, and well-paying ones. We speak a little unconventionally or take some shortcuts on words and you think to yourself "How dare they". If it wasn't so current it would be hard to even fathom the opportunities we give to others foreign born whether it be opening their businesses paying no taxes, etc. So as far as black people showing selfishness for things they should have, opportunities they do not get, chances that could change their lives ask yourself in that moment if they are really being selfish or are they being careful or uneasy about their future in the business that you work for? If we get to the point where these things even out or you can look across the room and see a true diverse culture then we can talk a little more about it. When you look around and see how selfish your organization has been with their choices of employees and why you will admit it doesn't make sense. You have put yourself in a situation where selfish takes on a different meaning and you realize a black employee is far from something that most organizations are selfish, unaccountable and uneducated without apology because they can be.

The easiest way to overcome the issues is following the guidelines of other companies based on government mandates. What black people want to know is do you really understand the underlying story behind those mandates or the true reasoning around them? That is what we should be opening our leaders' eyes too. How hard do you think it is to walk into work every day with a doubt of how long it will last or just saying thank you for the opportunity treating us as if we should be happy even having a job and knowing in the back of your mind this is as far as it goes and keep telling yourself "well at least I am out of the hood"?

If your approach is impacted when hiring and impacted when firing then continue to do more than read and watch what went on in the slavery days or the brief light bulb of a history class in high school. That just makes those with good hearts show pity. While our people suffered greatly for the very freedoms we have today (and would probably be extremely disappointed in our progress) our outlook and expectations have grown greatly since then which is even more visible now. Take some time to master your craft.

Take the time to truly get to know the people you encounter so that communications blossom and relationships build. Do not just buy them the hip hop cd, hats and Jordans for your kids and grandkids for Christmas without understanding more about the culture your kids might be leaning toward. If you rap like us, dress like us, sell our brands and omit our culture then at least be open as organizations to invest in our brilliance. Do not show us pity show us hope. Do not show us that hope because we are black show us that hope because we are worthy. Do not become afraid of those of us who become powerful because we just want to share that power with some who have had none for a very long time.

**Aggressive:** Think about the true meaning of aggressive. We are known to be in nature because of what you have interpreted. Aggressive to you is about what you read or see on social media. What you see as aggressive, we consider HUNGRY. We look around in these organizations and see a dominant force of white colleagues. If you ask me, we are not aggressive enough. We want to know more than others because we have not been included as much as others. We have more questions because we do not get as many answers. You turn our hunger into what makes you feel better about your lack of concern. You are afraid to have certain conversations with us based on the fact that you truly do not understand our culture. It is easier to classify someone's approach than to educate yourself on how to cope with it. Our nature is not about what you owe us, it is about trying to take back what is ours. Your understanding of aggression usually occurs when someone feels something is unfair. We have felt that way for hundreds of years. If someone feels more aggressive in their approach, we should ask them what is bothering them. The problem is most white leaders are afraid to. They are afraid of who they do not know. They are afraid of the confrontation that comes with leading someone different than they are. The fact that we are depicted as aggressive or angry proves your ability to make your mind up about the conversation before it even happens. This is why that hunger comes off as anger or aggressiveness.

If you continue to back someone into a corner they start to feel as if they have to protect themselves. There are very few blacks in the organization so labeling them makes it easier. If you are around more blacks you will realize that there are differences in every race and that all humans are subject flaws. White people just have the idea that our individual flaws as humans are because we are black. The worst part to that is that they will not admit society's flaw in putting us in that situation. Even when we are happy about something it may seem over the top. We do not get enough to celebrate, and our ancestors didn't have much of anything to celebrate. This allows us to raise the pride level when something is accomplished. These thoughts should be solely based on that accomplishment.

Unfortunately, our accomplishments come with the asterisk of being a black person. You expect us to get excited about small things because nature you assume we should expect less. We seem aggressive because you do not talk to or work with enough of us to paint a clear picture. Your ability to disregard us as everyone else has caused anger but do not think it is the first time we have experienced it. If our appearance or approach concerns you, ask yourself what you are doing to find a better understanding. When you're in a position of dealing with people, you owe it to yourself to make decisions based on a bulk of your work. How can you assess us when there is not a bulk of black associates? How do we know what you're expecting from us if you do not even know? You treat us as if we are an endangered species but one that is not of any concerning. Think about that and ask yourself if we are being too aggressive, or if we are misunderstood. Then ask if your organization is doing enough to prove to equality.

**Violent or Angry:** This is another word used often to condemn black people. If we say nothing or do nothing then nothing will continue to happen. If we do say something, we are violent or angry. It puts us in a position where we allow our voices to be silent so that we do not scare others. We are not a violent race. We are put in a place where violence exists. It is not the people that live in the ghetto that are violent. It is the system that continues to be violent toward us. Violence to us means life. Life does not happen in the ghetto without violence. We did not ask for our conditions they were imposed on us. If we talk back to a white teacher; we will never amount to anything. If we talk back to a white officer; we may be beaten or killed. If we talk back to a white leader; it almost feels as if we have disrespected our slave owners. Violence is what happens to us and what you read online or see on the news. Violence is a part of the way most of us grew up. When you put a bunch of people in a terrible situation under terrible circumstances, you will see more violence and killing. White people that are not willing to admit that should not be using the word. You are describing what we have escaped from but you will never allow us to escape it.

If we called white people ignorant because some of them show it regularly, does that mean all of them are? Pose the question about the person you meet. Do not answer it with opinions that you have not experienced. The silent backward ways society approaches this are fine with all. We get a little louder based on wanting to be heard, and your best go to is being intimidated because we seem like we are taking it harder than others. When you get a lot less of something, it hurts a whole lot more when it is taken away. Before you write us off as violent think about the violent way in which we have been treated for far too long.

**Defensive:** First question why is defense necessary? Leaders have to stop taking defense from their people as negative. How can a black person be defensive when we never seem to get on the offensive? Our lives are built around defending the very little that society has allowed us to have. You flipping these words to make us look like the bad guy is what we have felt forever. The admission here is that yes, we are more defensive than others. We have to be even if we do not want to. Most have the ability to let up on defense because they have others on the court or field that will help them. We do not have the same help so our defense becomes our offense. We have our youth joining the military to defend our country that does not even defend them. The point is, defense is thought of as necessary in most cases. Why are we aggressive or wrong when we get defensive? Do we have the right to be defensive based on the lack of education in your approach with us? Our consistency in being defensive is because your opposition against us has been the toughest offense we have ever seen. It becomes our natural wall based on how we have been treated and the unjust way in which it has been done. When a woman is in a bad relationship for a long time and they build a wall, it is ok. They become less vulnerable to the next partner based on what they went through. We have centuries of factual data to prove why we are defensive and the same people that give us the reasons to are the ones who question our stance.

When companies do not allow themselves to realize the difference in stature amongst their employees, it is a slap in the face. Your ability to ensure that everything is equal based on a code of conduct written ten years ago is a joke. Your ability to see through the defense and realize how good we can be on offense is your task and your responsibility.

**Welfare:** This is not a term that should be used to tarnish another group of people. It is a system built for the poor to help them live, but not as well as you do. You call it 'free money', we call it a product of the environment you put us in. Let me share how we feel about it. The welfare system is built for the minority community. It is your way of still being able to demean us for needing it and wanting thanks for getting it. Here we go: Thank you for building a working environment that is less conducive for blacks.

Thank you for allowing us the ability to take care of our families with the minimum. Thank you for labeling us as "on welfare and lazy". Thank you for allowing us to raise our families on a crumb of what you do. Thank you for not giving us the same resources and tools so that we can get welfare.

Ok you get it. You're asking us to feel bad because of the position that we have been in for years. You're asking us to be excited about an opportunity that you point the finger and say we should get a job. The worst part is when the economy struggles, black people end up struggling even more. Most of the jobs that take chances are smaller companies or "non-essential" businesses. The rich get richer and the poor do not get a damn thing. Do not build a society that excludes us and then point the finger at what we cannot do versus others. This is not a word that should be discussed in the corporate environment, but you should still be educated on the 'why', before you come up with a solution to the 'who'.

**Lazy:** This would be the word that stirs up the most negative energy. When a white person says this knowing that we started in the fields and doing jobs that white people do not even consider, it is proof that you do not respect our plight. We do not get the better jobs which means there are more in construction, warehouses and other jobs that require hard labor. How does that equate to lazy? We do not turn down jobs because we think we are too educated or that we are better than that job. You turn us down because we do not have enough education or because you think we are not capable of the position.

The understanding comes from seeing that one or two black associates that have made it. It is easier for you to say "If he/she did it, why can't others?" Our circumstances could be better or worse even as black people. There are different levels of poverty amongst white people but they act as if our ability to succeed bears on the few black candidates that you took a chance on. Their plight might be different than their counterparts. Our problem as a people is that it is easier to make assumptions about the unknown than to get to know them. It is easier to call us lazy than to admit our opportunities are different. The truth doesn't hurt it allows us to become more educated on the change that will make it better. The complete disaster amongst most corporations is that the most privileged do not understand their privilege. It makes it easier to make assumptions about what others can do.

As black people, we do get in our own way at times, but far less than white society has been in the way our whole lives. Looking around and seeing less of us doesn't seem to me to look like we are lazy. It seems as if we are not wanted. When the opportunities and resources are even, I will be open to your labels. For now, I will say that if we are lazy because we do not have better jobs, then you are even lazier for not doing what it takes to provide more opportunities for us. People get lazy because they know they have other opportunities that are better or something to fall back on. We as black people do not bask in those nuances so when you say 'lazy', we leave your interview feeling like we are still 'forgotten'.

**Uneducated:** Always start with the Why before you say anything. Are we uneducated or did we lack the resources to get a better education? You cannot blame an entire race for the neglect by yours. When I was young in the hood, having a high school diploma was worthy of celebration. Did America put us in places where it seems as if our education was not as important as others? Most were burdened with a high school experience where the pie chart was out and they had statistics on what happens to most black men and women. Why do we know that but do nothing about it? Why do we use the word uneducated when everyone does not have the same abilities to get that education?

Blacks who do have the opportunity at going to college, are then told the school that they broke the bank to go to is not as good or accredited as the more expensive colleges. There is no difference in the content so why does the actual college make a difference. This is another situation where some of us prove against the odds that it is possible to find out it is still not good enough. It has been proven in history that our education scared whites. They became afraid of how much stronger we would be with an education. That is the irony in using this term when describing black people.

I believe uneducated can mean a bunch of things. Some of us are too ignorant to even research and educate ourselves about the people they spend time with every day. Some can do more to educate themselves and decide not to. Some have all the resources necessary and do not care to meet society's standard of what the best choice is. Allowing yourself to label groups with this word is unacceptable, especially when our lack of education was not our choice but the only one given to us.

**Entitled:** Before you say this to a black employee, ask

yourself if we should feel that way. You cannot be entitled when you have no clue what entitlement means. How can we feel like we are entitled to something when most of what we had growing up we had to fight tooth and nail for? Here is how that interpretation internalizes with black people. We should be entitled to a lot of things. If we are making up for lost time that means we are owed a lot more than others. You are asking us not to think we should get a leader position with very few black leaders in the business. We should not ask for more as if we are used to getting everything we want. Entitlement does not make sense to people who have been limited their whole lives. If you ask me, the entire black population should feel more entitled to what they are not used to. When that happens, it will be harder for businesses to dismiss us. You have to build an environment that proves that promotions and opportunities are just as available to blacks as whites. Remember we do not see enough of us in these other positions, so thinking they are supposed to be ours seems farfetched. The fact that we WANT these positions without the proof of others achieving it should be applauded instead of labeled. Wanting something you have never had is not the same as getting everything you always want.

You could build an entire dictionary on certain phrases or words that are used in Corporate America that should not be used. Some of these words are not built to cause pain, but open wounds that you cannot fathom. They are not always said with intent but that is only because usually things that are done with intent are done after research or education. The goal is to understand that your meaning behind something does not mean the same to everyone you talk to.

It is necessary for good leaders to understanding how personal a word can be when talking to one person compared to another. Do not just get to know the ones that are easier to translate. I wanted to share some that have been more common in my experience to shed some light on the damage that can be done if we do not understand the impact our comments make. The best advice I can give is always know who you are talking to. Make sure you are educated enough for a rebuttal.

When you show someone that you understand their differences but treat them as one of your own, we are grateful. When you prove to them that you understand that there can be different meanings for things based on their circumstances, we feel respected. Our differences together are what makes our nation the strongest. Let's take a chance on translating this to our corporations having the strongest teams!

# Tips for Black Applicants

First and foremost, you have to believe and you are half way there. Do not take your other experiences into the next interview. They have to consider how long it will take you to recover if you talk down your prior employer. Your confidence has to allow the ability to believe you are equal. If you look around the office or the interview room, do not minimize your chances, regardless of what society tells us. That is an important reminder because it is the norm of most corporations right now. The fact that it has not changed should not make us think we are not worthy of the opportunity that is available.

Our mindset has to be stronger than others. We have debilitating circumstances to overcome that others do not. You are not just preparing for an interview. You are preparing as a black interviewee. This unfortunately means that your experience may mean that you do not bring as much to the table. I know this is not your fault but it is a reality. I want you to have the confidence to get a position that you want but the knowledge to know that you have to shine in other areas of an interview to make up for the experience you are lacking or the lack of resources available to you that seem like second nature for white people.

## Resume

This has become a very important part of an interview. My recommendation is to do your research on resume writing. Reach out to a friend or associate for help updating your resume. There is a lot of information on line that can help with this process. It is about more than just updating it with the last job and sending it out. This is not just a job resume but a personal resume that needs to spark the original nerve of the person reading through the resumes.

Think about how many times you applied or sent your resume and never got a response or phone call. While I do not believe in this way, it still allows the person scanning the resumes to make decisions on whether you should even get an interview. This is your calling card and making sure it tells the true story is important, as whether you even get a chance to interview for an opportunity may depend on the way your resume is written. There are platforms to use, templates that can work and you can look over other examples you can find on line to educate yourself on how to put together a visual that will make those who look over it more intrigued to talk to you.

If it is a phone interview, be prepared to speak to what is there, but most of all what is not there. You are selling yourself and you should not take shortcuts. Do not allow where you worked previously to be a distraction. It does not matter whether you liked the job or not. You have to be accountable for your part in everything. It allows us to piece together what we want to be better in the next position. Most importantly do not trample on the last company you worked for. This gives the new business a sense of bitterness or that you will talk about their company the same way if things do not work out. I have always said that if you do not have anything nice to say the best thing at times is to say nothing at all. The past should not dictate your vision of the future or what is possible. Prepare you resume so that it is flawless.

## References

This is harder for black candidates than others. Unfortunately, we grew up in a place where it is harder to find the type of references that the corporations are looking for. Success is in the eye of the beholder. We will spend weeks trying to justify whether our references meet the corporate standard or whether they will be looked down upon the same as we are. The great part to this is that they do not know who the person is beyond a reference. They are not checking white or black for references provided. You know who you can trust or count on. You know who has the same mindset, wants or needs. That is a strong enough reference to feel good about putting their name down.

Find a few that will be strong references for you who

have a strong passion like you do. The people we know that we would ask for a reference are just as good as any other. They just struggled with the same things we have always struggled with equal opportunity. If you have good relationships at other jobs; ask for a written letter of recommendation. It does not matter how important the actual job was in terms of public perceptions. The thoughts of your leader and your performance at that job are the most important thing to the interviewers who will call them.

Do not overdo it. Be careful of trying to build a resume you cannot substantiate. I know our idea of doing it is so we have the same odds as others.

The risk is that you will become exposed if it is found out that you cannot do what you say you can or even worse, finding out that you do not have the experience that you provided in your resume or interview. If you feel you have to lie to compete, it is probably not the job for you. The more truth we give them the more they will understand that their guidelines or necessities are not missed, because we didn't feel like it is important. Let your dedication and hard work prove to what they may see as risky and show them that the lack of our creativity is what is lost the most in a lot of organizations. Focus more in the interview on how willing you are to learn and how passionate you are about taking steps toward that. What you lack, you can gain based on your passion and openness to something new.

# Forget About the Perfect Job

I want to make it clear that this in no way means that I do not want you to aspire to anything you want to do or accomplish. The goal is that we at times take what we have lost over time and start to think we are entitled or owed something. Honestly it is true that we are owed something (as I clarify above), but of most corporations do not see it this way. Our entitlement and bitterness will only make things even harder.

Most do not realize what is wrong and right based on their experiences. The goal is to get your foot in the door. This part of the discussion is more around our younger generation that starts to wrap their mind around what they want blinding themselves to the reality of society. Our younger generation has seen a glimpse of what can be. They tend to use that in the job preparation or expectations. If you meet the criteria, I would never tell someone not to go for the job they want. I would warn you, however, that regardless of whether you meet the requirements, you are still black and unfortunately that makes a difference.

Sometimes the job you want starts with the one you didn't. The goal of this discussion is not to think beneath what you are worthy of. I am just asking that you be as honest about your limitations as you are about your successes. The perfect job would entail perfect people to do that job with. That is the part that is out of our control so our preparation is different than most. I want people to believe that they have the ability but understand the circumstances in that process. My point here is that regardless of the position, it is a way to get our brilliance in the door and prove our worthiness. It will also paint the picture for the job you actually want.

## Stop Disqualifying Yourself

We tend to disregard most opportunities based on what we read or see. We are automatically staying in a place of comfort, and why? It is not your fault you did not or could not afford a better education. It is not your fault that the company you are seeking is asking that you worked at others like it previously. If you say no, before anyone else does, then you have already lost the battle. If you believe you are not worthy based on requirements set by the company you are applying for, maybe it is not the best fit. We are told by everyone to focus on the things that we can control. Well, being hired while black should not be out of our control. I understand you are walking in with less than others have, but that is based on requirements. It is what people cannot see or measure that brings out greatness. Beyond that, we can either run from the obstacles or let them defeat us before even trying. The requirements set by organizations are built from data that are purported to show what will provide the best candidate. It does not say that it is impossible if you do not meet those requirements.

Why should we believe we are not capable because we did not achieve the level of schooling that someone else has? How do we change the unemployment rate for blacks if we are holding them to a higher standard than you knew was available to them? Remember, white business owners:

it is not what you say it is what we see and what you do that frustrates us. The torture in figuring out why things are so different should not have fuel added to it by denouncing us before we walk in the door. Believe in your blackness and the creativity that comes with that. Use what seemed like disadvantages your whole life to your advantage. Pressure is a daily thing for us and a pressure that most could not fathom.

Compared to the world we come from the things we face in the workplace are nothing. We always talk about risk well, our risk at times was just walking out the door. Tougher environment? Our environment was the toughest. The ability to overcome obstacles? Some cannot do it at work we had to do it to survive. Do not limit your blackness because the jobs you apply for do.

## Confidence and Personality

Do not let anything get in the way of your confidence and personality. Your understanding of tragedy and will to win cannot be matched by all of the schooling and experience in the world. You have to allow this to shine through. Do not get me wrong, in an interview you have to understand the audience so that you do not get too comfortable in the process. I do not care what the qualifications are; if I get the chance to interview, I believe I am the guy. The difference is I believed it even when I didn't get certain jobs.

I would not allow specifics to get in the way of what I thought I was capable of. Even if I did not get the position,

I made sure the capability was understood. People that lack confidence and do not meet qualifications can be tuned out in an interview easily. Our personality traits are where we stand out. Our smoothness and suave ways can win over a room. Those that usually do not qualify for a position will attack it as if they already know the outcome. Our mindset has to overcome the norm and focus on changing it with our abilities, creativity and hard work. Remember, the people that truly make a difference in the building have a lot less college degrees and experience. They do have passion and will that have been disregarded for centuries. Walk into the interview with the confidence to change that.

## Dress for Success

This is another obstacle that can be harder for us than others. Even with second hand stores it can be hard to afford what society feels is necessary dress attire for an interview. We have to respect this if we want to join their firm. Forget about the fellas calling you a sell-out or an Uncle Tom for dressing the part. The reality is if they had the opportunity, they would do the same thing, or they only talk about the ones that make it which proves they do not care to. We all have to be open to change. That change does not change your culture or make you less then. It just means that you understand that there are certain things that we have to conform to so that we are as professional as others. The goal is not to let the corporate culture turn you into someone you are not. You have to stay true to who you are mentally so that you can overcome the real obstacles in the workplace. Clothes, however, are put on and taken off every day. They are not insisting you have to dress that way when you are not at work.

I will be honest though, once you get used to it, there is a different feel of success that goes with that. You find that you are not doing it because you have to; but that you feel more successful in the process. If you look good, why should you be mad because it is not what you usually wear? Do we ever eat things we have never eaten before? If you have sleeves or arm tattoos you should wear a long sleeved shirt. Remember, this is the initial meeting. At some point they will be out and it will be irrelevant. My point is to give them a chance to judge the canvas before they see the complete portrait. We have to prove that we are not scared of change and know that the outfit does not make the man, the man makes the outfit.

## Get Some Rest

This is more important than you think. This should be part of your daily plan but the night before an interview is the most important. You want to be at your best. You want to make sure that your preparation to be at your best starts the night before with being rested and ready. Take some time to think about the interview and gather your thoughts. Make sure you count the dollar signs in your sleep and wake up ready to take on the world.

# Research your Opportunity

You have the ability to use this to overcome some of the other areas that may be less impressive. You really should research any company that you wish to apply to. It will show more interest in the interview on your part, but the key is to make sure this is a company you are interested in. What are the possibilities to advance? For this purpose, I want you to do it to show immediate gratitude for the opportunity. If the interviewer knows that you have done your homework it shows them that your interest is real and the passion you show in wanting it even more real. Talk to them about things that you researched on the internet. You always want a company to feel as if you already believe in their product or service. If there is a description of services or products on the website, speak to what you found interesting about the these. Look at new acquisitions and mergers. Find a few articles on the website so you are up to date on the vision of the business and what they are looking to accomplish. The easiest way to overcome possible deficiencies in your experience and qualifications is to prove to them that you're passionate about the company's products the direction they are going in.

There will be other applicants with more experience but that experience does not weigh as well in a different industry. They will not do the necessary research, relying on their resume to do the talking. Ask your interviewer what they like the most about their time with the businesses. They keep that one at the tip of their tongue but you're asking about their favorite experience, which shows you are interested in a future. Keep them focused on the current and the company because it is easier for the interviewer to let their guard down and become interested in the conversation.

Remember you could be the tenth interview that day. Does experience really mean the candidate is better? What if their experience was face to face sales and the job was for a phone salesman in a totally separate industry? Is someone with more education always the best choice? What if their schooling was for a teaching degree? This ability to circumscribe the opportunity for most, to find what you think is the best has never worked to its expectation. I want black candidates to understand more than they are expected to. I want them to know that sometimes showing that you really want to be a part of an organization, depends on your understanding of what they do and your interest in that. There is something about raw talent that excites me. You can mold it and change the game with the opportunities it brings. Skill can be taught but we continue to make this as easy on the trainers as possible by trying to find people that fit perfectly. The true focus of teaching in any aspect is to understand your students' strengths and limitations to better plan their success.

Our experience frequently tells us that even though we hire those with the most experience; they may not be the best fit for your company! GIVE US A CHANCE!

## Greeting

Remember, do not let the things that are out of your control break you. You have to focus on what you can control and not the things that may prevent you from getting the job. Find that internal passion and blow them away. Greet them and ask them how their day is going before they even ask you. Courtesy is an easy ice-breaker. Smile and show you are there to begin a new journey. Do not frown or dwell on how long it took. Shake hands with the interviewee. If it is a man then shake his hand firmly and look him in the eyes with confidence. If it is a woman, it is imperative that you look them in the eyes. Shake their hand with firmness so you gain their comfort. Do your best to find your balance and sit up straight. Always look at the interviewer throughout the interview. When you are in a new place, there will be a lot of distractions.

Try your best to stay true to the task at hand. That can mean very little to some but a new life with hope for the future for most.

## Be Passionate

Do not ever let anyone tell you that passion is not the most important asset to have. I do not mean at work I mean in LIFE! Passion cannot be mistaken. It cannot seem like something else. You cannot fake being passionate about something that can change your life. Some missed opportunities can never be regained. The only way to win is already knowing what it feels like to lose. This is all we have done. Even though everyone knows that, we still do not get a pass. That is why we have to allow our passion and hunger to come out to sway the corporate minds from the norm.

I know for a fact that there are true interviewers out there that will hire passion over experience at times, because I have been around and led many that do. I hope in some way I was able to change the thinking of some with my actions. Passion is not about a situation. It is about a way of life. It does not turn on or off nor can you allow anything to turn it off. There will be more obstacles than wins for blacks. That is a fact! Every time one of them gives us a chance, we have the ability to open the door for a few others. Do not play into the stereotype of who they think we are if you are struggling. Stand up and think about what you went through to get there. Then ask yourself if it is really that serious.

Our mindset as black men and women has to reset on a daily basis. I still get on the elevator at times after twenty-two years and white employees look at me as if I broke in. We do not accept it but we learn to live with it. Many great black men and women fought hard for change and were only heard by other blacks. We cannot change white people, they will have to agree to change and for the right reasons. Until then your passion is about balling everything up that you have gone through and realizing you have beaten everyone and everything that has beaten you.

Be passionate about even the small things because you never forget where you came from. Passion is about knowing you are a proud black man or woman regardless of how the rest of the world sees you. With that kind of passion, you can turn heads, close their eyes and make them hear you. Yelling and screaming works for some and I stand by their ability to do that too. My goal was to get to a place and tell a story that can change lives because BLACK LIVES MATTER. You have to learn to love something more than other people do not want you to have it. If you thrive in passion, even your failures become learnings. Black people already deal with a lot without being given anything. Do not let that fire go out because it can take a long time to light it again. They can take opportunities, but passion stays with you, whether stay or go.

## Take Your Time with Answers

Try not to get caught up in the "who sounds like who" conversation. The truth is the most educated you will make the best impression in Corporate America. Think about your answers and take your time answering questions. One of the best pieces of advice is to admit when you don't know something. Trying to piece together an answer to suffice can only make the situation worse. Most interviewers will ask a drill down question based on your answer. The key is to be passionate and honest with the answers you can give. They do not want to be fooled; they want to be absorbed by the interviewee. Make sure you ask them to restate the question if you need clarity. Speak clearly in the interview so that your answers are heard and felt.

Prepare questions for the interviewer. Ask questions

that will bring out their passion. Ask about their plight in the business. People love to talk about themselves in those positions. DO NOT ask monetary questions. I know that is on your mind throughout the entire interview, but you have to refrain from making it seem like it is a deal breaker before you are offered the job. The money will be discussed before an offer is made and you still have the ability to accept or not. The goal is to ask questions that show you are intrigued and looking for a career and not just another job.

## Interview Closure

This is your lasting impression the one that actually gives you the nod over some very close competition. Wait for the interviewee to stand at the end of the interview. Make sure you ask for a card so that you have the interviewer's information. When you stand up, shake hands again and show that passionate smile. Thank them for the interview and extend a final thanks by letting them know you hope to be a part of the team. This is where you walk tall and be proud of yourself regardless of the decision.

Once you are home send another email to the interviewer using the card they gave you. Thank them for the time and information and most of all their consideration. If you do not get the position, think about sending another email. In this email you can ask for feedback to work on, which is always impressive. You can also express that you would like them to keep you in mind for future consideration. You wouldn't believe how impressive follow up can be.

# Overcoming Snubs

This is and always will be the test of strength for black employees. I have heard a lot of stories that clearly show our chances compared to whites. I decided early on that I was not going to believe that I did not get opportunities based on being black. I would admit that some of my culture and personality traits may have measured in. Here is the thing I am not going to be mad about something they cannot say out loud. They cannot tell you that you didn't get the job because you're black. So I was not going to waste my ability to think forward for something that could not be said out loud. I just went out of my way to perfect everything else so they had no excuses the next time.

Allowing yourself to feel like you didn't get an opportunity because you're black is buying into the fact that it continues. At some point when you are knocking everything else out of the park the truth will prevail. There are too many opportunities lost based on how we condition our minds. We cannot allow the neglect from a few white people to change the greatness we can learn from the good ones. I am not saying this is not an issue in Corporate America because it still is. I am saying that I will never allow myself to believe the beautiful black part of me was the reason I was rejected. Being snubbed is already tough to swallow. Do not take on the burden that we have already had to carry forever as the reason. In business, we face obstacles on a daily basis, so do not take on more unnecessary obstacles or thoughts.

Focus on the things you can control and being black is

not one of them. You want to prepare solidly for the next opportunity if you expect things to change. I have seen it happen to a lot of people obviously mostly white men since that is Corporate America right now. There are times where the most qualified does not get the position. Other times it can be an external move when you have already proven you can handle the responsibility. Regardless of the reason, never allow yourself to believe you were denied because your black is not brilliant enough. IT IS!

# SUMMARY: THE TWENTY-SIX-YEAR JOURNEY OF A BLACK LEADER

I have had a long successful career over more than twenty-six years in the corporate world. That came with a lot of pain and agony. It also came with the long-time friendship of a lot of great people within that time. I wanted to try and give an understanding of what black associates are dealing with in the modern world. I do that hoping that most already know about our history, slavery and the most terrible times for blacks. I did not want to diagnose history and state all of the facts that most already have. You have either been taught some history through school or you do not educate yourself because you do not care. My experiences could never compare to what our some of our black compatriots have gone through. They do however, continue to prove that things have not changed as much as whites would like to pretend they have. Your continuous approach to find a statistic to prove differently is exactly why the needle has not moved enough. It is a scared determination that makes us feel as if you never want to us to become equals.

While I believe I met more good people than bad in my career, almost 90% of them never understood white privilege. Unfortunately this is the part that allows them to think it is ok to make comparisons. They appear to assume that, because they become friends with a black person, which I assume this gives them the right to make definitive statements or define a race. The intent is what they stand by, but our pain gets pushed back even farther every time a comment is made. Every time someone speaks without knowledge, we feel more alone. Every time a joke is made, we think about our ancestors and why they suffered so much to become a punchline. In some ways, you are halfway way there if you are able to befriend someone that others will not. It means you are open enough to get to know someone different than you and realize the differences are not as big great as you thought. These are the ones that who are willing to eat lunch or be seen with someone of color and not care what others think.

However just because you are able to do this, this does not give you the right to make black people the butt of your jokes. How do you act around your black friend or associate when your other white colleagues are there? Do the jokes become easier to say?

Do the jokes of others become funnier when other white colleagues are there? Either way you are responsible for being that open person that will stand up for your friend.

You cannot be afraid to address others when you hear or see something wrong. Forget about corporate guidelines and the stress by them to do it. Think about yourself and how you would feel. The 'golden rule' is an easy way to live life. If someone is treating someone with disrespect or in a bad way, it is wrong. Why would it bother someone any less because that person is black? You have to be honest with yourself on why you ever thought that. I am not asking you to beat yourself up over it. Your honesty will prove to you that there is no good reason to treat us differently. If nothing else, you should be on board with the fact that things have been unjust and unequal for a very long time. The comfort of those who make these comments is obnoxious especially with the understanding that it is not ok in the workplace. I had no specific socioeconomic advantages. When you hear people say things like "You have to sound more vanilla", you realize that the lessons necessary are far from understood. I have tried to dispose of the fact that my life was so hard. I think that is because when you spend a lot of your time around too many people who are disinterested in your plight or culture, you figure it is not as big a deal. Based on the stories they tell their lives would have been heaven based on how I grew up. I was afraid to be honest because their worst stories were better than I could have ever imagined growing up. I realized that most of them had never even driven through the places I grew up by accident. While some I knew was pure ignorance it helped me understand that white people just do not understand.

The question, however, is why they don't understand. If everyone is talking about how hard their life was going through six years of college, you figure they could never understand your pain. The "Why bother?" is where white people have to become more active.

You start to swallow your pride a little and allow things that you know are not ok. It is the slave mindset of believing it is alright to treat us as less worthy of rights and respect, as long as you open the door and let us in.

My goal early on was to keep my job. This is the mentality of most black men or women who get a door to open. Most of them allow the extra comment here and there, because they don't see any alternative. If they protest, they'll be considered to be difficult, and their corporate career will be cut short. White people look it as a way to tell more jokes. We look at the consequences of saying something about it and ending up back in the hood. The reason racial comments and jokes are so common in the workplace is because blacks are always outnumbered. The bigger reason is because if every black person feels like I did, they are not going to say anything. We also do not expect anyone else to speak up either. The commonality of conversation within the workplace comes from what is common to most involved. If one person out of twenty speaks up with a different approach, it is always brushed to the side. Think about always being that one person of the twenty. It becomes less necessary for our voice to be heard. This happens because we start to truly believe it doesn't matter or the general population have made it clear it is not acceptable or wanted. How can you uncover the brilliance of the minority in your business if we do not continue to open up to our ideas as well?

I remember being so caught up in the atmosphere of the offices. I would look in groups of more than a hundred and see one other person. Where I grew up, you would pack your bag and run if those were the odds. I thought I was being punked at first and someone was going to tell me it was a joke. Let me add that it was a group of some of the most loving people I have ever spent time with but without more of me how could they truly ever except me. I thought to myself listen with this kind of money and opportunity, you have a chance to provide a foundation for your family. Then I was amazed by the fact that I was just going to be talking to people all day. No construction anymore, no figuring out what the next move was. I was given an opportunity to do something different than others were and I have not taken it granted since. There were programs in place to help in efficiency areas that were necessary to the business. I was able to go back to college after six kids and get my degree with the support of my company and some of the funding to do it. These are small things that companies can do to prove to those who may need more support that they get it. More than that, they feel comfortable enough to raise their hand. I immediately became the man I have always been the guy that wanted others to win more than he wanted to win. Companies didn't understand that growing up in the hood, those wins were far and few. I was excited every time I heard that someone from where we grew up finally made it. It was always darkened by a larger amount of tragic loss and broken dreams. I knew it was impossible to transform to the average employee or change who I was at heart. I did know that I would have to hide a lot of it. The fact that I could not be as passionate as others about my culture or what I loved was the hardest. I was not afraid to share regardless of how others felt. I was just smart enough not to scare people with the real truth if I wanted to keep feeding the family. We all know that the conversation changes in the corporate world based on the audience. If you have ever told a joke and even the black man laughs do not think that gives you the ability to use it in front of another black person. Instead of the black guy and his laugh; think about the pain behind that laugh. We have to reassess at times and ask why he is allowing that. We look at the paycheck and weigh the odds. Hopefully this will help you understand why saying the wrong thing is wrong even if the black person laughs with you.

It makes us question our blackness and what our friends back home would think. I realized many times over during my career that I was dealing with far more than I should have to. The painful thought thinking back is that what I was hearing in the business was not half as bad as what I heard white people say growing up. Black people will artificially make light of one situation versus another because it is NOT AS BAD. This is why it is so important for white people to start standing up for us as well. It will allow us to focus more and put up with less of this in the process. It will make us feel we are a true part of the team and its success.

You see, when we cannot plan your life when we're a young teenagers based on resources you we do not have we think you are doing us a favor by giving us a chance. You think you are lucky because there are not many like you instead of wondering why. Instead, you wonder if you do ask, whether there will be one less black person. I became very educated in a short time as far as the politics involved so it was even harder for me to put up with what I had to at times. This cultural shift makes black men and women continue to battle internally with staying true to who they are and adapting to a new culture. Some black men and women get caught in the trap. They lose who they are in who they think they can be. The problem is that it gets even lighter the higher up the chain you go. That loneliness I felt was something I felt my entire career. It wasn't based on my colleagues; it is and always has been based on the system. Do not take our comments personally if you are not willing to endure our pain.

After a few years in the business, my family had grown tremendously. I now had six beautiful children. I wanted to enjoy the blessing of being able to raise them in a way I did not experience. This was the toughest part of my career. Now I had six reasons why I had to continue to be silent or put up with the nonsense that goes on in the office, and six more reasons to deal with the ongoing jokes. I was doing all that I could to outwork everyone around me.

Another trait amongst those of color that corporations need to pay more attention too is demonstrated by the following. I was one of the top performers in the nation in sales while I was still a temporary employee. I started to take notice of the fact that I had to learn to deal with outworking and outperforming others and still not being rewarded. I do not mean individual accolades or achievements. I had great experience and acknowledgment throughout the years. I am talking about the new opportunities the ones that fewer blacks have or none do.

In twenty-six years, I never had a black manager. That is a long time fighting to even believe it was possible. I spent over thirteen years on the phones without even being asked what I aspired to do. Others already had a plan in place on what it would take to get there. It seemed as if they didn't expect me to want to be a manager or aspire to those positions. There were a few reasons this part of my career was so hard. The pressure to deal with unacceptable circumstances as a black man is one thing. That same pressure and thinking of all of your babies in the process makes it six times as hard. I felt like without all of the same degrees there were times where I was the smartest in the room. The problem is no one asked so I figured I wouldn't tell. I continued to see the same movement in positions especially management. Those movements did not include black representation.

I believe I made it my mission to change the culture of a business I loved to work for by changing the narrative. I stopped paying attention to why there were no other blacks in the room. I started paying attention to the minds in the room. I did this to gain the knowledge to stay in that room instead of complaining about not being allowed in. I did it to share that knowledge with other black men and women so that they understand how to overcome. Most of all even though I was thirteen years into a sales career, I knew I was worthy of a shot to lead. I wondered if anyone black would get a chance so that it would give me more hope. At some point I stopped wondering and started asking.

I dressed pretty casually, based on the fact that my first positions were phone sales. I will never forget the most honest conversation I have ever had at the job. It came from someone who over time became a true mentor in my career. She said "Listen if you want these people to take you serious, you have to think about a way to lose the gold chain and the earring". It seems rude to say right? I thought it was the sincerest thing any white person beside my mother had ever said to me. Her honesty allowed me to take it as a lesson instead of a stereotype. I even knew that some would have taken it that way. I also knew that she had my back and proved that regardless of how I was treated by others. She became a hero of mine in the business world and truly allowed me to believe that I could be a leader in a business where there were very few black employees. My answer to her honesty was, "If you give me a manager position, I will take the earring and gold chain off tomorrow!" She had the ability to realize that, based on the corporate status I needed to change my image to be taken seriously whether fair or not. If I hadn't received that advice, I might still be a sales rep because after a decade or more, you stop believing you will get a shot. Did I absorb all of those jokes for a good paycheck? I refused to let that happen! Let me reiterate no leader ever told me that I could not move up or that opportunities would be available. I also was never asked if I wanted to be one either. It was not even two months later that I came in with a two-piece suit, no earring, no chain and the passion to change the lives of those I lead.

The first conversation after that was not congratulations for becoming a leader. It was congratulations for becoming the first black leader at that time in the business. Think about that the pressure I put on myself and what I had to go through to get the chance. Immediately you get the pressure of being the only one. The second part of that conversation was that I would never succeed not in so many words, but the gist was clear.

I was given my first outbound team and seventy percent % of that team was on final warning for performance. Human Resources even stepped in at some point with concern about whether I had been set up for failure with this team. The problem is I knew that if I did not grab this opportunity, who knows when the next would come or if it would? I would prefer to take the risk with a team that was struggling than to go back to struggling in my mind about why I was not a leader. This was my shot to show and prove myself. I never had it easy growing up so that is where you turn your disadvantage into your advantage. I lived a pressure-packed life so this wasn't pressure it was a challenge to make a group that felt lost feel like they could do something they hadn't yet. Sound familiar? Hope is all we want. In an organization we want our teams to succeed. We do not want part of them to succeed. This was not a group of black men and women.

This was a group of different genders that lost their way. I didn't start to think like a leader when I got the position. I started trying to motivate and inspire my colleagues before I became a leader. I proved my work ethic throughout my career so asking for my team's best makes sense. I never led a team where I rooted for some over others. I built families that rooted for each of their family members. I didn't run teams where I had to deal with racism because I led by example in supporting each and every one of them because that is what a true leader does. If I did not understand their culture, I would do the research so that they didn't feel left out. I would ask about significant others and children because I wanted to lead with the objective of helping them achieve it.

The ability to lead others to success beyond your own individual success is leadership. You see I understood sacrifice walking in the building years before my opportunity to lead others. It wasn't hard for me to root for others because I understand what it is like to have nothing. I understand what it is like to want more for others like me. We have always been in a situation where we are rooted for less but always find a way to forgive and keep rooting for others. It is in our nature as black human beings. We have been through so much more than everyone else, but forgive more than anyone else does. We know how to build others up that feel down because we have been there over and over. We know what it feels like to think you are no longer important to society; not just the organization. The compassion we have to carry is just so that we are not overwhelmed by what we want but cannot have. The anger you see is because we realize no matter what the approach, those that could listen don't! Those can do something about it won't.

Let's get back to my first team. There were a lot of conversations and learning who they are and what they want. We put a plan together to achieve those things. I was given the ability to move the team to the other side of the building by themselves. We started to have daily huddles so that my appreciation for all they did was understood before the day begins. Instead of just working for the business, they started working toward a purpose. They stopped focusing on themselves and learned from each other. They came together as a group of individuals and built themselves into a family. That team that was such a risk to take on became the team I was always the proudest of. I actually earned the top award for leaders that year with a team that no one thought would be there another year.

Over the next ten years I won trips to St Martin, Bora Bora, Sicily, Portugal, Hawaii and Costa Rica. I became a senior manager and decided to use everything I learned from great leaders along with the things I wanted to change that I learned from mistakes. I allowed myself to learn that at a pace that did not include race. I wanted to become what others didn't see so that they had a true example for their aspirations. I did want other black associates to have a strong role model.

This does not take away the systematic realization that we do not feel as important and our culture is not as relevant. This is about companies who reward those that deserve it to realize that if some do others might too. Companies might see the staggering difference between whites and blacks in the business and be honest enough to say it is a problem.

As you move into senior positions you believe your voice matters more. You make sure you are heard and you are more confident in your suggestions. Even though you have made the climb it took more time to recognize me than it took for other white counterparts to get a leadership position. Unfortunately, you realize it was easier when you were silent. It is easy to uniform our passion which I talk about in our meaning versus yours in a prior chapter. You think we are being aggressive but we have been shut down our whole lives. It is passion and it should be taken as that. Your being intimidated alters your ability to listen to us. Thinking we are going to become violent keeps your guard up. We are people whose feelings get hurt times ten. We have experienced people talking at us our whole lives. Your thought process around who we are makes you run from confrontation. It could have actually been a good conversation. This put me in a situation where my passion was lost at times and I stopped following my gut. One white man after another giving me hard scores about traits they have never taken the time to understand. That is the equivalent of saying I do not care about your struggle. I am going to treat you just like everyone else. That is the easy answer because most of "everyone else" looks just like you. We have to again allow ourselves to be silenced because of your anticipation of what may happen.

The reality of whether something is salvageable lies in good overcoming bad. The fact is that you met one good person for every three you would see. If you love someone and the relationship is falling apart, most times if the better times are more than the worse; you are willing to give it a shot. We do not expect to be in a relationship, or at least not a happy one; if we are consistently weighing the odds. This is the constant pressure put on black men and women simply because you do not give enough of us a chance to realize what you are missing. We have to set an example of the few in the organization and do our best to leave most of our culture at the door. That means you are accepting a very small group of associates and asking that they conform to your structure. That is like someone coming to work without pants. If what we wear or the way we talk seems different to the point where you think it is wrong it is a clear suggestion that you have not engaged with most blacks your whole life. If we have to meet your standards just to walk in the door then it becomes one more step backward for us.

Now those who know me know that school was a breeze to me. I didn't miss honor roll until eleventh grade when I was becoming a father. I went back for my Business/Marketing degree and finished with a 3.97 GPA. I never questioned whether I was smart enough to be in the room. I did know that I had to find the resources to become twice as good as everyone else in that room. The problem was my darkness makes others uncomfortable. Even with that in mind, I wanted people to focus on the light.

I do believe my career would have gone different if I would have just agreed with everything and challenged nothing. You see the higher you get the more you realize you have to be content with what you have accomplished. I had to stop worrying about why one after another would jump me in positions. I had to focus on building something I never had throughout my career a sense of unity, a family of team members from all different origins and beliefs to stand together each and every day to celebrate one another. It was the most genuine thing I have ever been a part of.

I became a senior director and I would speak at every huddle to draw some sort of inspiration. I have crafted the art of speaking in a way that makes it visible and real. I speak to my teams about hope and hard work but more about believing in themselves and each other. We have to stop leaning on preparing employees to be better at their job or the next one in the business. I prepare my team for life. The young one's gain knowledge and understanding.

Those of us with history need to be reinvigorated even after years in the business. I wanted to show the love and support I had growing up in my neighborhood with no father around. I wanted to prove that if you have been treated unfairly, you do not have to let it consume you. I wanted to do something in a way that the company had never seen and I accomplished that. I didn't do it for a raise or to get a promotion. I did it because with every platform you can perform or you can light up the stage. I do it so that if it changes the day of one person out of two hundred; I have made a difference a difference that is above and beyond the leadership standards.

I realized that I could make change at the highest level without the promotions. I have been one of the most successful leaders in the business based on the numbers since I became a leader. I want to be able to tell my grandchildren that I took a platform of managing people and used it to bring out the best in people. I showed them the type of belief they needed to win. I did that when no one ever did it for me; whether young or old. I did it because showing support and inspiring someone can also change their feelings for the next black man or woman they meet.

I have had some of the best times of my life working in the corporate world. A lot of them changed my life for the better. I have met some of the best people that are still in my life to this day. I never want to sound ungrateful for all I have been able to achieve. The tough part is that there were tons of unfortunate situations, whether there was intent or not which stick with me. They never go away; they just build as the years go on.

There are a lot of white associates who love their place of employment but never had to deal with any of the common racism that goes on. I have watched people follow the lead of others knowing it was wrong. I have had discouraged black associates who look to me to be their voice. Remember I can only be so loud before I am thought of as aggressive. We have to stop being afraid to educate our employees on the struggles of our team and how we can work together to make them better. When I stopped looking up and learned how to lead up in the process I became even better. I have led some of the best senior leaders in the business for over a decade. They were able to catch up to me before I was able to catch up to anyone else. I know it doesn't make sense but it never does and you stop expecting it too. You can be the best at what you do and still be glossed over every time. I used the smoke from that fire to fuel me. I wanted to build leaders better than me so that titles stopped mattering so much. I lead the way I taught tae kwon do over two decades. I will give you all you can handle regardless of your belt color. I was in the martial arts for ten years before I got my black belt which is similar to how much time I spent on the phones. I allowed the experience to push me and my teams to the highest limits instead of allowing bitterness over how long it took.

My true focus became my teams. Whenever those teams changed it did not change the help I would still give to others in that process. People ask me personally and professionally how I can be so positive. The reality is there is nothing in life that was harder than getting to the opportunity I received to move forward. I wanted to build a team that wanted to come back every day whether it was good, bad or indifferent. I wanted a team where each individual would battle through the last day with the team already over goal. I wanted a team where they cheered on each individual and did all they could to help those who were struggling. I received a team and many after that have become the ones who inspire and motivate me every day.

I understand what I have done with my opportunity, not because I have not missed a month in over ten years but because of the fact that all I have given to the business has been given back by the people I have worked with. Every time they accomplish something new, they want to share it and celebrate. When you live to motivate and inspire, you have to be inspired at times. There were many times I was not inspired looking up, so I decided to look in front of me. I put my feelings aside so that I could lead with strength and set the right example.

My goal is not to point fingers at corporations, it is to make them more aware and to ask them to get better. I wanted to take all the pain and anguish and turn that into a platform to make people of all colors better. I wanted to show people that our strengths are our ability to overcome obstacles, and see past the racial prejudice. I wanted to take the bitterness of losses or snubs and turn them into opportunities without allowing myself to believe it was because I was black.

I hope that all I have gone through will help others find the strength to become exactly who they want to be even in a world that does not want to accept them. When you are alone you draw more attention. I mean you wouldn't believe things I have talked to my leaders about more than the true impact I make daily. I realized I am unorthodox and unconventional so that is different. I would build a firm with people like that. I took all of the pain and all of the love I have received over the years and found a way to appreciate all people at a level that will always supersede the tough times. As business owners you have to take the next step. Your voice is helping but your actions are waiting. Only you can change what is reciprocated by the employees. The jokes are less funny to everyone when it is reiterated as unacceptable from the top down. You are already going to take the most heat based on your diversity levels and programs in place. Do you know what kind of flash this can give you company? It is only a risk if you are doing it for the first time. In this case, it is just not done enough. The past will show you the brutality in how we were treated, but the present will as well if you do not open your eyes.

It is no longer the norm that needs to be status quo. The companies can talk the talk but it will be obvious if they do not walk the walk as well. A true leader is not afraid of the consequences of taking a chance because their people are what's most important. Think about your stories on the boat or yacht. Then think about how many of those conversations you have had with other black associates. We continue to follow the lead because we have been chasing our tails for a very long time. We just keep hoping that the true leaders stand up so that we have the same opportunity to move forward All I ask is that you truly do your research. Look at some of the same staggering numbers around diversity for your business and take a stand to change the common denominator. We have the ability to educate ourselves using just a thumb print, so why are whites so uninformed about their black counterparts? There are so many resources to use and yet so little knowledge. You have to forgive us for thinking that if you do not know by now, you may just not care to know.

I wanted to write something about the current status of corporations keeping in mind the obstacles of blacks in that process. It is not to say that corporations are bad, it is simply to remind the owners and decision- makers that they can do more. The statistics prove it. The reality of everyday business shows you the difference. The goal is to focus on the unheard. Most racism is not only understood but history gives us enough information to make good decisions moving forward. It is the in between that we have to be more structured and united on the things that seem ok to most because it is the norm.

I have been able to stand tall and proud and hold my ground. I have been able to do that surrounded by all white leaders for over two decades. All the way through my Senior Director leadership I have been the top performing leader in the channel. I out worked or worked smarter than most that I competed against. I raised six kids and got to see the world with my wife. Most of all, I took a platform and used it in a way to change lives not just inspire employees. So, if a few up top decided not to see the core of who I was, then it gave me the opportunity to show it to hundreds of others.

Regardless of what anyone has always thought I ALWAYS WIN. If you cannot control my mind, you cannot stop my progression even when it seems like I have lost. I guess I am saying that once you get a lot of good from something, being snubbed doesn't hurt, it keeps you sharp!

I mystify myself in a prism of passion when it comes to leading individuals. I live to honor the ones I love whether lost or present. I live to be an example to my children and to other young black men and women. I live because I survived a tough life. I live to be the father I never had. I live to be the leader I never thought I could be. I lived to be able to experience what my life has become.

I am calling you out as leaders, executives and owners and asking you to be the breath of fresh air that so that you can be the pioneer of change. That is what is needed for Corporate America to be in the forefront of this charge and show at a high level that our Corporate America includes all of us.